MEL BAY'S DELUXE
FINGERSTYLE GUITAR METHOD

BY TOMMY FLINT

A stereo cassette tape of the music in this book is now available. The publisher strongly recommends the use of this cassette tape along with the text to insure accuracy of interpretation and ease in learning.

D1379556

FOREWORD

This method has been brought into existence to acquaint the student with some of the requirements of today's fingerstyle guitarist and to enable him or her to develop the skills necessary to meet those requirements.

If conscientiously studied, this method will provide the student with an enhanced technique, a thorough knowledge of the fingerboard, adequate note reading ability and a basic foundation of good musicianship.

The techniques utilized in this method have evolved over years of study, practice, performing, and teaching, as well as being influenced by the masters of fingerstyle guitar.

Many thanks to Merle Travis, Mose Rager, Chet Atkins, Mel Bay, Bill Bay and the many friends who have offered encouragement and help, and have been a source of inspiration over the years.

This book is dedicated to my friends, Jim Stark and Cliff Harper, with whom I have traveled many miles, through both the dark lonely night and the golden days of summer.

THE GUITAR PARTS

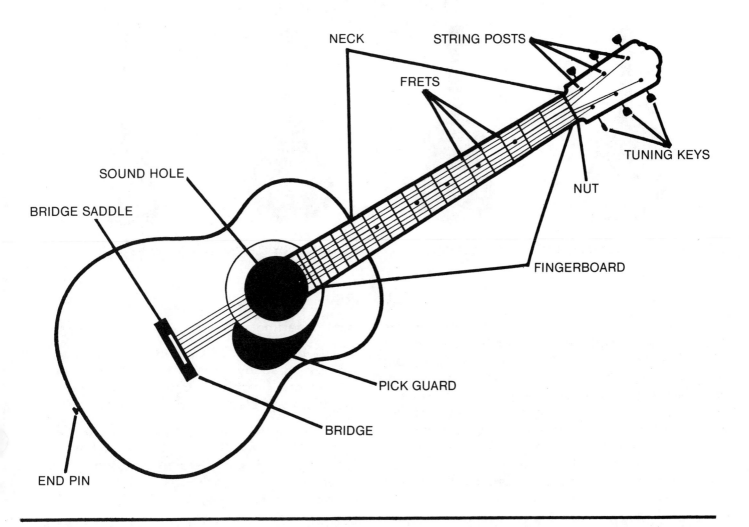

NECK

STRING POSTS

FRETS

TUNING KEYS

SOUND HOLE

NUT

BRIDGE SADDLE

FINGERBOARD

PICK GUARD

BRIDGE

END PIN

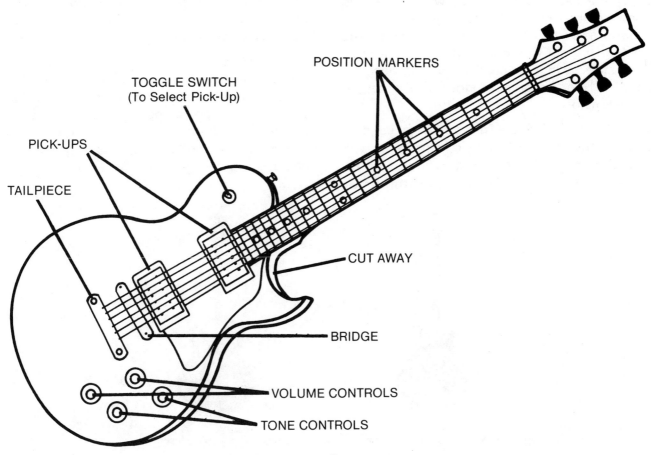

POSITION MARKERS

TOGGLE SWITCH
(To Select Pick-Up)

PICK-UPS

TAILPIECE

CUT AWAY

BRIDGE

VOLUME CONTROLS

TONE CONTROLS

TYPES OF GUITARS
USED IN FINGER STYLE

FLAT TOP ACOUSTIC or FOLK   CLASSIC   HOLLOW BODY ELECTRIC   SOLID BODY ELECTRIC

GUITARS

FLAT TOP ACOUSTIC—This is a very versatile guitar and is widely used today. It can be adapted to almost any style of music from strumming folk songs to Travis picking, bluegrass, single string, and Chet Atkins style. It could possibly be considered the foundation of country music and the Nashville sound. It is possible to use almost any kind of strings on this type of guitar. Steel, bronze, silk, and steel or ball end nylon strings can be used. This guitar is characterized by the round sound hole and flat top.

CLASSIC GUITAR—The classic guitar is characterized by the round sound hole, wide neck and fingerboard, and nylon strings. The wood in a classic guitar is usually lighter than in other guitars in order to bring out the tone of the nylon strings. Never put steel strings on a classic guitar, because the wood will not be able to stand the stress or increased tension.

HOLLOW BODY ELECTRIC—This guitar is used in almost all styles of modern music from folk, rock, and jazz to country. The tone and quality is determined by the electrical pickup and amplifier control setting.

SOLID BODY ELECTRIC—This is the guitar found in most of today's rock music. The sound possibilities are unlimited depending on the pickup, amplifier and electronic devices used.

Both the acoustic and electric guitars are used by some of the greatest finger style guitarist. The type of guitar to use is strictly a matter of personal judgement as to which type would be best suited to the music being performed.

SEMI HOLLOW BODY ELECTRIC—This type of guitar is used a great deal in modern country music and rock. It has essentially the same possibilities as the solid body electric.

ARCH TOP ACOUSTIC—This type of guitar is not used a great deal in finger style playing, as the mellow wide tonal range of the round hole flat top is usually preferred. This instrument is used widely as a rhythm guitar in dance bands. The arch top and "F" holes produce a bright penetrating tone that "cuts" through the sound of the band.

SEMI HOLLOW BODY ELECTRIC   ARCH TOP ACCOUSTIC

STRINGS

NYLON STRINGS—Nylon strings are used on classic guitars. They have a soft mellow tone and are easy on the fingers. They stretch quite a bit and need to be tuned quite frequently. They will stay in tune much better after they have been on the guitar for a few days. Ball end nylon strings can also be used on flat top or folk guitars.

SILK AND STEEL—Silk and steel strings are excellent for finger style on the flat top folk guitar. They are usually easier on the fingers than the steel or bronze strings. They cannot be used on electric guitars as they will not pick up sufficiently.

STEEL STRINGS—Steel strings are used on the electric guitar. The wound strings are sometimes wound with nickel winding. We recommend fairly light gauge strings with a wound third for finger style on the electric guitar. Sometimes very light or slinky strings with a plain third are desirable for playing blues or rock on the solid body electric.

BRONZE—Bronze strings can be used on the flat top or folk guitar. They usually have greater volume and more brilliance then the silk and steel. The light gauge strings should be used for finger style unless you are using finger picks. Then it would be possible to use a heavier gauge. These strings should not be used on the electric guitar.

BRASS STRINGS—Brass strings are very similar to the bronze and are used for the same types of music. The tone is somewhat more sharp or bright. Brass strings are not to be used on the electric guitar.

FLAT WOUND—Flat wound strings are made for the electric guitar. They are wound with flat wire (no grooves or ridges) and are very smooth and soft to the touch. This also eliminates finger squeak (the finger sliding on the wound string). However, they do not have the brilliance of the round wound string.

FLAT POLISHED—Flat polished strings are standard wound strings which have been ground and polished until they are smooth. There are flat polished strings for both electric and acoustic guitars.

Again, the type of string for you is a matter of personal choice and depends of the tone desired for your preferred style and your requirements for ease of playing. The strings should be changed regularly in order to retain a good tone and accurate tuning. Old strings sound dead and will not tune true. The life of the string depends on how much you play and whether or not the strings are wiped clean after each playing session as well as the quality of the strings.

HOW TO HOLD THE GUITAR
THE CLASSICAL POSITION

 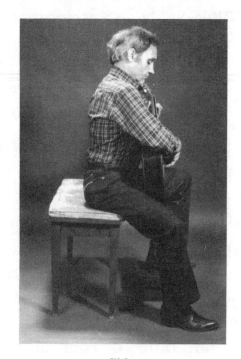

Front   **Side**

In the classical style the guitar is held on the left leg. The left leg is elevated by placing the left foot on a footstool.

The guitar sits on the left leg and is held against the body by the right forearm.

Both hands should be free to move and should not be used to support the instrument.

The neck of the guitar should be held at approximately a 45 degree angle and the nose should be directly over the twelvth fret, as shown in figure 1.

Sit erect and hold the guitar in a vertical position as shown in figure 2. In other words do not let the guitar lean back at an angle.

SOME OTHER POSITIONS
THE CROSSED LEG POSITIONS

In both of the above positions the guitar sits on the right leg and is held against the body by the right forearm.

THE ELEVATED RIGHT LEG

The right leg is elevated by placing the right foot on a footstool.

The guitar sits on the right leg and is held against the body by the right forearm. Keep both hands free.

THE FLAT FOOT POSITION
BOTH FEET ON THE FLOOR

In this position the guitarist sits on a chair or low stool with both feet on the floor. The guitar sits on the right leg and is held against the body by the right forearm.

THE STANDING POSITION

In this position the guitar is supported by a strap over the left shoulder, as shown in the above photograph.

The guitar is held against the body by the right forearm.

SITTING ON A HIGH STOOL

This position is favored by some guitarists. The guitarist sits on a high stool with the left foot flat on the floor. The right foot in placed on a brace or round of the stool, which elevates the right leg. The guitar sits on the right leg and is held against the body by the right forearm.

HOW TO SELECT A GUITAR

Select your guitar from a reputable firm. Seek the advice of an established teacher or experienced player before making your selection.

The type of guitar you select will depend upon the style of music you are interested in-Country, Folk, Rock, Classical, etc. (See page 4.)

The strings should be fairly close to the fingerboard so they will be easy to depress, but they should not be close enough to buzz or rattle against the frets.

The neck should be straight and free from warp or bow. However a slight bow at the half way point of the neck is desirable. It should be just enough to slip the edge of a sheet of writing paper between the string and fret when the string is held down at the first and twelfth frets.

The instrument should tune true in all positions. (All the way up the fingerboard.)

TUNING THE GUITAR

If you are a beginner, it would be logical to have someone — your instructor or a friend who plays, tune the instrument for you. The knack of tuning the guitar accurately is in most cases acquired after the student has been playing for a period of time. A great deal of experimentation, practice and patience will be required until the ear has developed to a point where it is capable of determining the exact pitch of the strings.

There are various methods of tuning such as: by octaves, harmonics, chord inversions etc. The three most common methods are shown below.

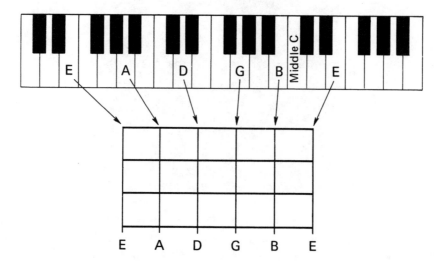

The six open strings of the guitar are the same pitch as the six notes shown on the piano keyboard. The first string is above middle C. The other five strings are below middle C.

THE PITCH PIPE

Each pipe has the correct pitch of the individual string.

If both piano and pitch pipe are unavailable:

1. Tighten the 6th string until you get a good clear tone.

2. Place the finger on the 6th string behind the 5th fret. This will give you the pitch of the open 5th string.

3. Place the finger on the 5th string behind the 5th fret to get the pitch of the open 4th string.

4. Place the finger on the 4th string 5th fret to get the pitch of the open 3rd string.

5. Place the finger on the 3rd string behind the 4th fret to obtain the pitch of the open 2nd string.

6. Place the finger on the 2nd string behind the 5th fret to obtain the tone of the open 1st string.

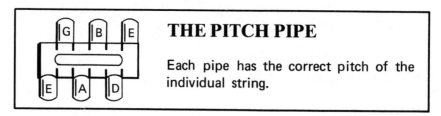

Now the guitar should be in fairly good tune and the chords will sound pleasing to the ear.

RIGHT HAND NOTATION

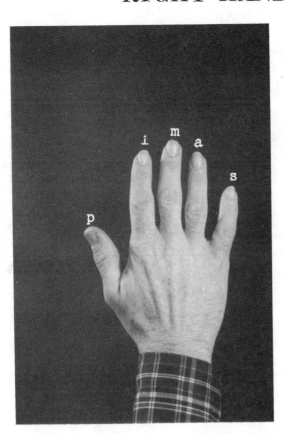

Fingers of the right hand will be indicated by the letters

p - THUMB or PULGAR

i - INDEX or INDICE

m - MIDDLE or MEDIO

a - RING FINGER or ANULAR

s - LITTLE FINGER

The letters indicating the fingers will appear above, below or to the right of the notes in musical notation and/or the numbers in tablature.

LEFT HAND NOTATION

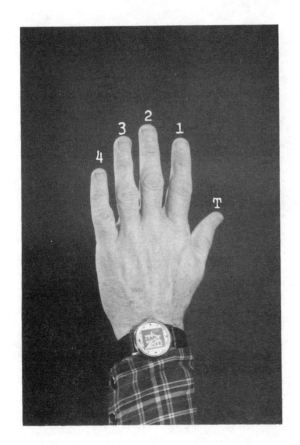

The fingers of the left hand will be indicated by numbers. The thumb will be indicated by the letter T. The numbers will appear in chord diagrams and above, below or to the left of the notes in musical notation.

THE THUMB PICK

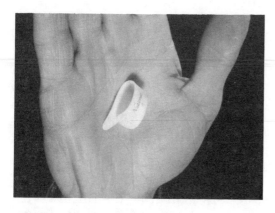

THE THUMB PICK

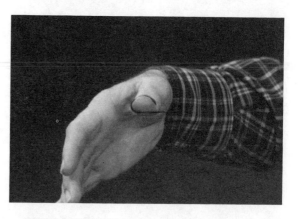

HOW THE THUMB PICK FITS

Although <u>no</u> picks are used in the classical style, I would recommend using a thumb pick in order to get a clear ringing tone and also a good solid thump on the bass strings. This is especially important in the Atkins and Travis styles and also Blues and Ragtime. The thumb pick is also very useful in playing fast single string styles such as fiddle tunes and bluegrass. Down and up strokes.

Thumb picks come in many shapes and sizes. Most are plastic, however metal picks are available. Choosing the correct thumb pick is a matter of personal choice. I think most guitarists prefer the plastic pick. It is probably more adaptable to all styles of music.

The pick should fit on the thumb as shown in photograph upper right. It should fit firm enough so as not to turn around on the thumb or slip off. However, it should not be tight enough to be uncomfortable.

FINGER PICKS

THE FINGER PICK

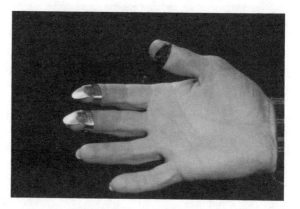

HOW THE PICKS FIT

Finger picks are <u>not</u> recommended. However they may be necessary on heavy gauge steel strings. For most people, finger picks seem to "get in the way" and limit the playing performance. Although some very fine guitarist use finger picks, they have probably been playing for many years, or in some cases were banjo players before taking up the guitar. Again, whether or not to use finger picks is a matter of personal preference.

The picks go on the fingers as shown above right. I have seen some guitarist use the picks on top of the fingers, over the nails and play down strokes. This seems to be very awkward and quite unnecessary.

THE RIGHT HAND POSITIONS
THE CLASSICAL POSITION

Only the thumb and fingers touch the strings.

The thumb or fingers do not touch the top of the guitar. The hand and wrist should remain relaxed. Use thumb and fingers only. Do not use wrist.

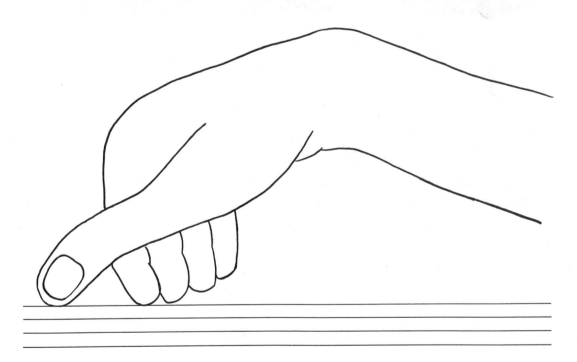

STRING

The above drawing shows the correct wrist position and the angle at which the thumb and fingers attack the strings, as viewed from above.

THE RIGHT HAND POSITION FOR STYLES
OTHER THAN CLASSICAL

Let the hand hang in a relaxed position over the strings. Now place the thumb on either the fifth or sixth string, the index finger on the third string, middle finger on the second string, and the third finger on the first string. Now your hand is in the proper playing position. This may vary with different styles, but basically this is the correct position.

Remember to relax.

The wrist should remain stationary at all times when playing fingerstyle. Use the fingers only. Just curl them in toward the palm of the hand as if making a loose fist.

Do not use the wrist.

The right hand before picking the strings.

The right hand in the closed fist position after picking the strings.

FINGERNAILS

RIGHT HAND

The nails should be filed to the approximate shape or contour of the finger tips. They should extend slightly past the finger tips approximately 1/16. It is advisable to carry an emory board to keep the nails smooth and in playing condition.

Grade 600 sandpaper may be used to smooth the nails.

Generally speaking, it is not wise to play heavy steel or bronze strings with the bare fingers. You may wear the nail down and cause gaps and notches to appear in them.

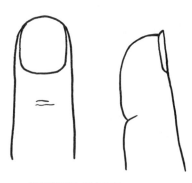

RIGHT HAND

THE LEFT HAND

The nails of the left hand should be filed very short so as not to interfere with holding down the strings and making chords. They should also be very smooth so they won't hang up on the strings and cause sloppy technique.

HOW TO PLUCK (PICK) THE STRINGS

Do not bend here

Bend here

The thumb should not bend at the first joint. If you bend the thumb it will get in the way of the fingers and you will have very little control over it.

The thumb should remain straight at all times.

TIRANDO – THE FREE STROKE

Used in Classical, Country, Folk, Blues, Ragtime, Travis Style, etc.

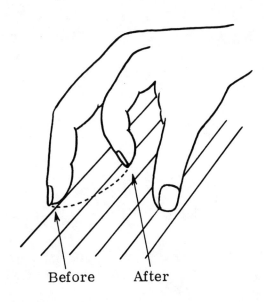

Before   After

Place the thumb on one of the bass strings. Place the finger on the ① string. Pluck the string using the nail and finger tip. Curl the finger in toward the palm of the hand in a semi circular motion.

The same movement is used for the i, m. and a fingers.

APOYANDO – THE REST STROKE

Used mainly in Classical and Flamenco for playing single string passages, scales etc.

Place the thumb on one of the bass strings.
Place the finger on the ① string. Pluck the string using the nail and finger tip. Do not bend the finger.

Let the finger come to rest against the ② string.

Repeat this procedure on the ② and ③ strings.

The rest stroke produces a loud tone.

Before   After

15

THE FREE STROKE

BEFORE PICKING   AFTER PICKING

THE REST STROKE

BEFORE PICKING   AFTER PICKING

THE LEFT HAND POSITION

Place the fingers firmly on the strings very close to the frets. Bend the fingers and use the finger tips, unless you are holding down more than one string with the same finger. Then the finger should lay flat on the fingerboard. Generally, the ball or pad (never the tip) of the thumb should remain on the back of the guitar neck. Do not bend the thumb. Occasionally it may be necessary to use the thumb on the bass strings on some chords. In this case it will obviously be essential that you bend the thumb.

If the strings buzz or rattle, slide the fingers up closer to the frets. Remember to keep the fingers arched so they will not touch other strings and deaden them.

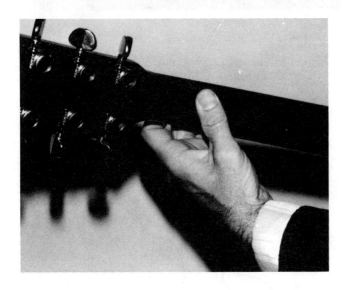

The correct position of the thumb
Classical position
Also used for single string picking

Position of the left hand when using
the thumb on the bass strings.

The correct position of the thumb
Back view

The correct position of the thumb
Side view

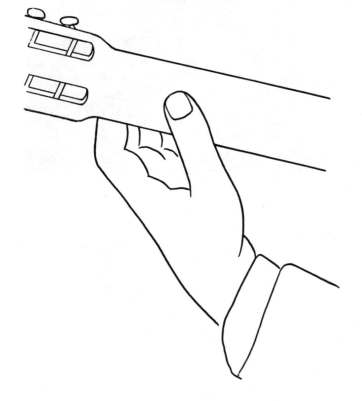

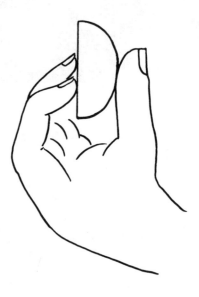

THE FINGERBOARD
CHORD DIAGRAMS

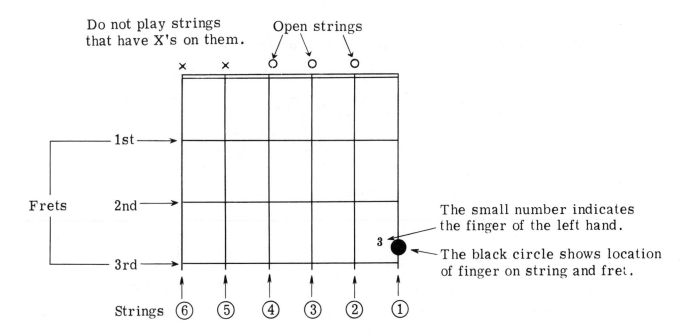

Do not play strings that have X's on them.

Open strings

Frets

1st

2nd

3rd

The small number indicates the finger of the left hand.

3

The black circle shows location of finger on string and fret.

Strings ⑥ ⑤ ④ ③ ② ①

The vertical lines are the strings. The horizontal lines are the frets.
The encircled numerals are the string numbers.
Open string = Do not touch string with the left hand.
Do pick string with the right hand.

HOW TO FINGER CHORDS

When making a chord, the fingers should be arched so the finger tips are pressing the strings straight in toward the fingerboard. Care should be taken that no finger touches a string other than the one it is depressing. The fingers should be placed firmly on the strings, as close to the frets as possible without getting directly on them.

THE RUDIMENTS OF MUSIC
THE STAFF

The staff consists of five lines and four spaces numbered upward as shown below.

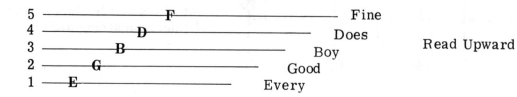

5th Line	
4th Line	4th Space
3rd Line	3rd Space
2nd Line	2nd Space
1st Line	1st Space

The lines have letter names

5	F	Fine	
4	D	Does	
3	B	Boy	Read Upward
2	G	Good	
1	E	Every	

The spaces also have letter names

5		
4	E	The spaces between the
3	C	lines spell the word "face".
2	A	
1	F	

THE CLEF

This is the treble or G clef.

Guitar music is written in this clef.

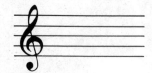

This sign will be written at the beginning of every piece of guitar music.

The staff is divided into measures by vertical bar lines.

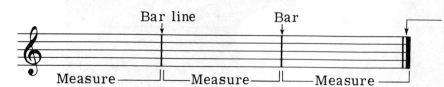

Bar line   Bar

A double bar means the end of a section or the end of a piece of music.

Measure ——— Measure ——— Measure ———

NOTES

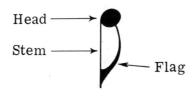

Head ⟶
Stem ⟶
⟵ Flag

THE WHOLE NOTE

This is a whole note.   The whole note receives 4 beats or counts.

𝅝   𝅝

Count   1   2   3   4

THE HALF NOTE

This is a half note.   The half note receives 2 beats or counts.

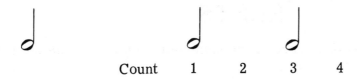

Count   1   2   3   4

THE QUARTER NOTE

This is a quarter note.   The quarter note receives 1 beat or count.

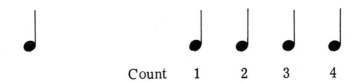

Count   1   2   3   4

THE EIGHTH NOTE

This is an eighth note.   The eighth note receives one half (1/2) beat or count.
Two notes for 1 beat.

Count   1   &   2   &   3   &   4   &

THE TIME SIGNATURE

At the beginning of every piece of music is a time signature. The top number tells you how many beats or counts are in each measure. The bottom number indicates the type of note receiving one beat.

$\frac{4}{4}$ Beats per measure

The quarter note receives one beat.

Some time signatures

$\frac{4}{4}$ $\frac{3}{4}$ $\frac{2}{4}$ $\frac{6}{8}$

C Signifies common time which is the same as $\frac{4}{4}$

The time signature is placed after the clef sign.

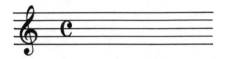

RESTS

A rest sign indicates a period of silence of the same duration of time as the note to which it corresponds.

Whole rest   Half rest   Quarter rest   Eighth rest

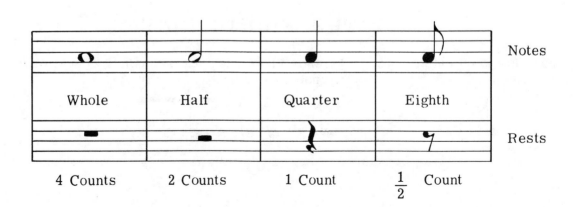

LEDGER LINES

When notes are written above or below the staff, they are placed on, or between, extra short lines called ledger lines.

SOME EXERCISES IN KEEPING TIME

1.   Hold the guitar in one of the positions shown on pages 6 through 9.

2.   Slowly and evenly count 1 — 2 — 3 — 4 — 1 — 2 — 3 — 4.
3.   Space the counts as evenly as a machine or a clock.
4.   Now, tap the foot on the floor on each count.

| 1 | 2 | 3 | 4 | 1 | 2 | 3 | 4 |
| Tap | Tap | Tap | Tap | Tap | Tap | Tap | Tap |

5.   Next, pluck the ① string on the count of one only and sustain the tone, or let it ring for four beats.

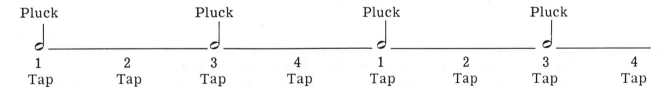

6.   Next pluck the string on the counts of one and three.

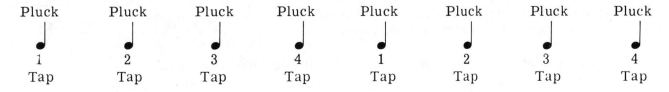

7.   Next pluck the string on all four beats.

23

TABLATURE

Tablature is an easy and convenient method of determining the exact location of each note on the string and fret. While not a replacement for note reading, it should be used as an aid until the guitarist has progressed to a point where it is no longer necessary.

The tablature will appear throughout this book directly under each note of music, showing exactly the string and fret on which the note should be played.

HOW TO READ TABLATURE
THE FINGERBOARD

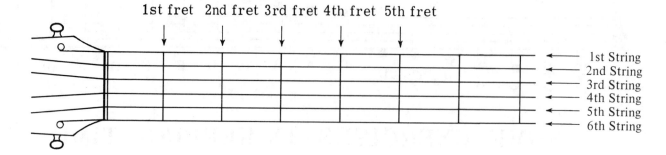

TABLATURE

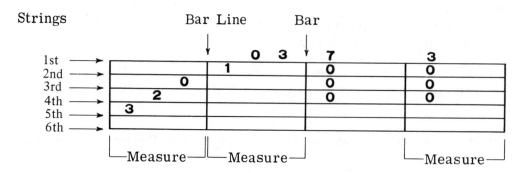

The lines represent the strings of the guitar. The numbers represent the frets. ○ indicates open string. When a number is above the top line, it will be played on the first string. When a number is above the second line from the top, it will be played on the second string. etc.

In the example above, the number three in the first measure indicates the third fret on the fifth string. The number two indicates the second fret on the fourth string. The ○ indicates the third string open.

In the third measure, the number seven indicates the seventh fret on the first string. The second, third, and fourth strings are open. The four strings will be struck simultaneously as a chord. When the numbers are arranged vertically they are always played simultaneously.

A small curved line between the numbers indicates they are to be counted as eighth notes. In other words, the first number is on the count and the latter number is on the "AND" or half way between the counts.

EIGHTH NOTES

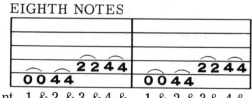

Count 1 & 2 & 3 & 4 &   1 & 2 & 3 & 4 &

For sixteenth note rhythm the curved line will arch over four numbers.

REPEAT SIGNS

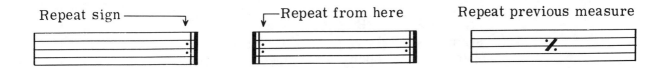

Repeat sign ———→   ┌—Repeat from here   Repeat previous measure

D.C. Go back to the beginning. D.S. Go back to the 𝄋 sign.
D.C. al Fine = Repeat from the beginning and end at Fine.   Fine = The end
D.S. al Coda = Repeat from 𝄋 play to the sign ⊕ then go to the Coda.

The End ┐   The end of a section ———→

FIRST AND SECOND ENDINGS

In the example below play through the first ending and repeat the selection.
The second time, skip the first ending and play the second ending.

First   Second

The Accent mark > above or below a note indicates that it is to be accented, or picked harder.

THE CRESCENDO SIGN ———————

The cresendo sign placed over a passage of notes indicates that this section should gradually increase in loudness.

THE DIMINUENDO SIGN ———————

The diminuendo sign placed over a passage means to gradually decrease or diminish in loudness.

THE FIRST THREE STRINGS OPEN

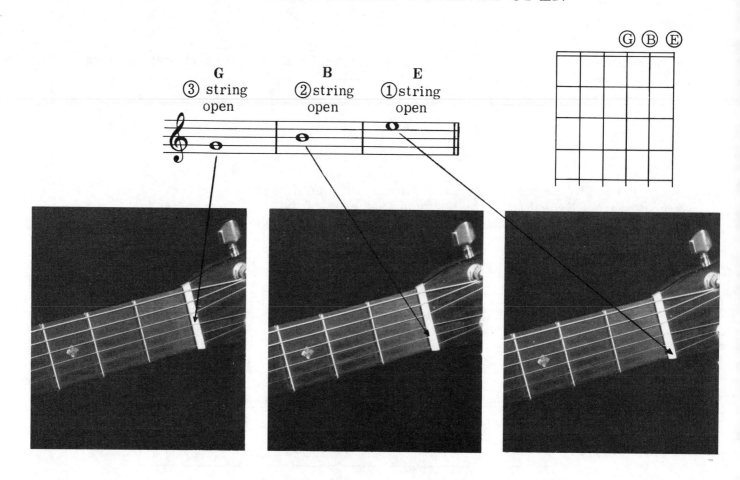

WHOLE NOTES

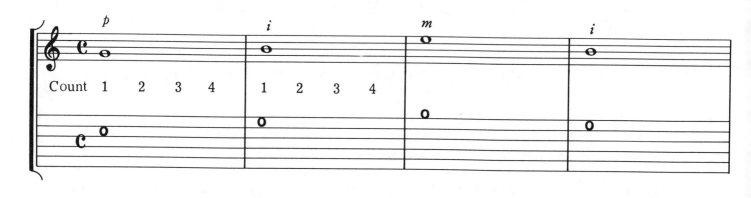

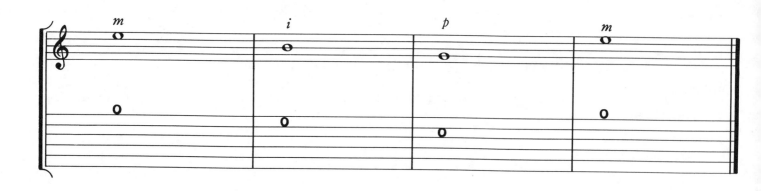

HALF NOTES

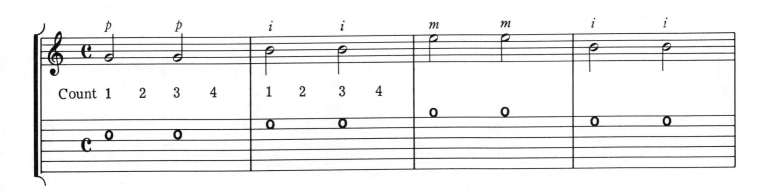

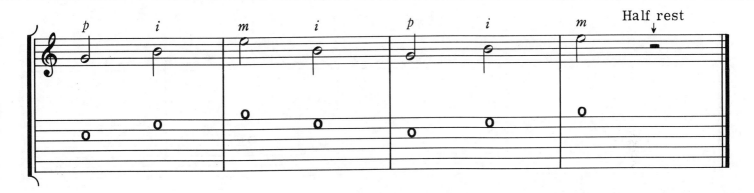

QUARTER NOTES

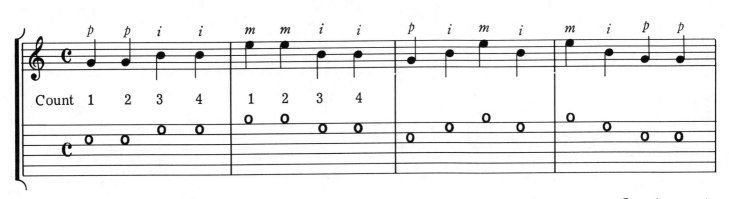

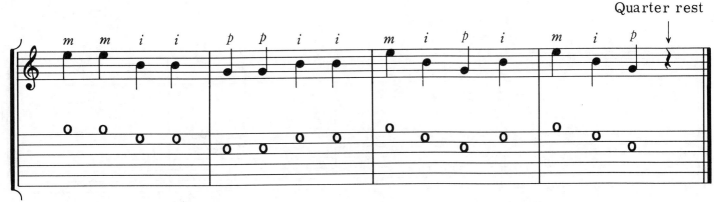

THE OPEN ROAD

Tommy Flint

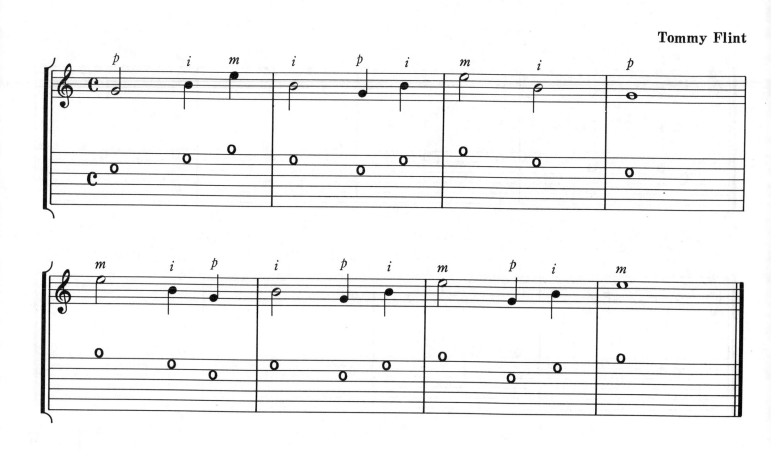

GET IT ON

Tommy Flint

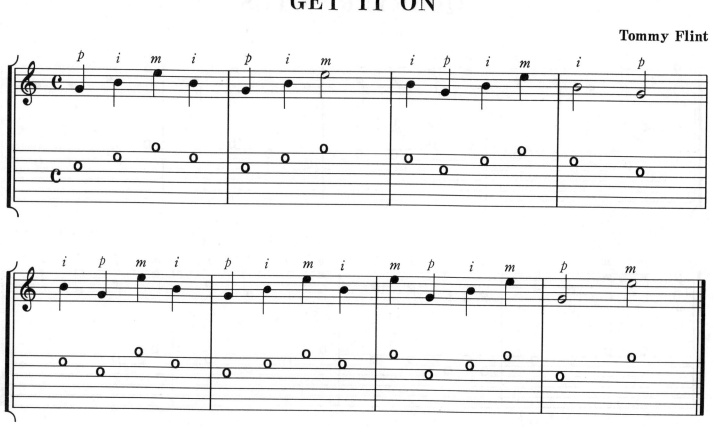

TWO NEW NOTES ON THE ① STRING

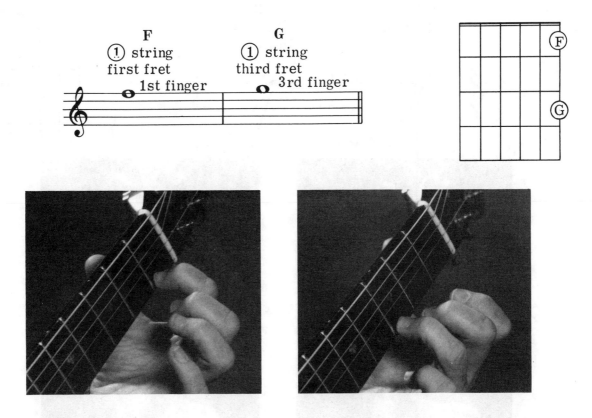

USING THE TWO NEW NOTES WITH OPEN STRINGS

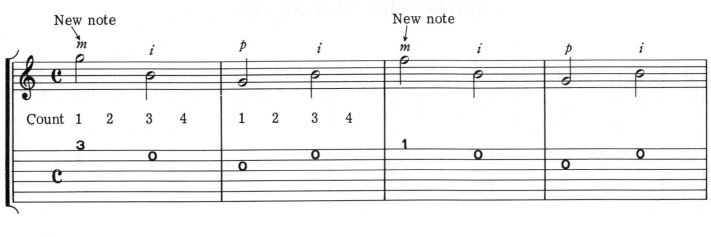

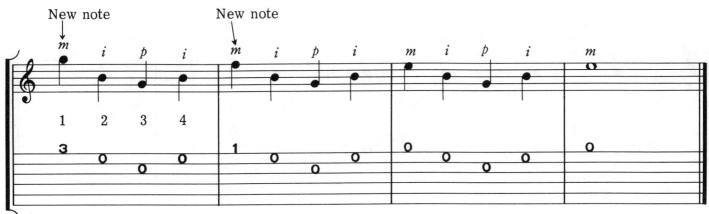

TWO NEW NOTES ON THE ② STRING

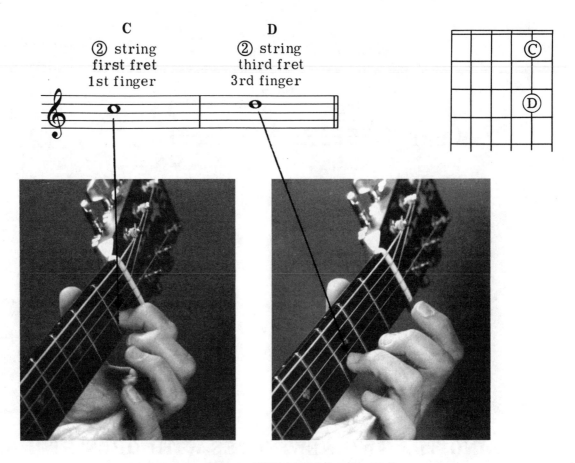

C
② string
first fret
1st finger

D
② string
third fret
3rd finger

USING THE NEW NOTES

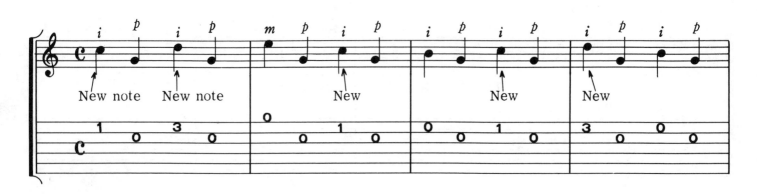

FLY UPON THE WALL

Practice slowly and evenly.
Instructor should play accomaniment chords.

Tommy Flint

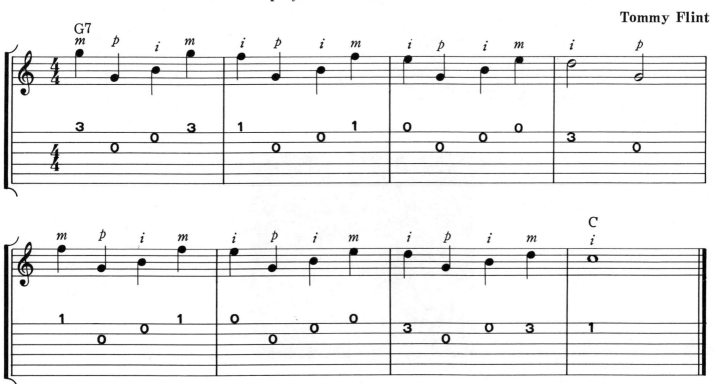

ROLLING ON

Tommy Flint

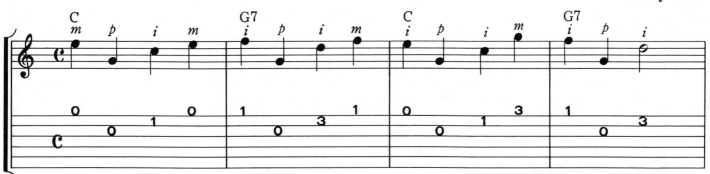

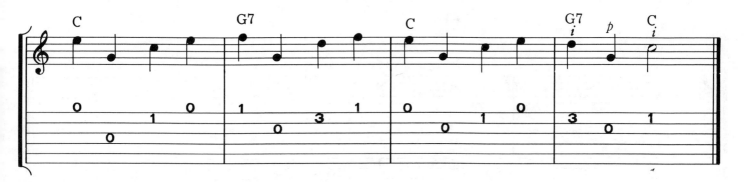

Recommended —
Mel Bay's

THEORY & HARMONY FOR EVERYONE
By L. Dean Bye

A NEW NOTE ON THE ③ STRING

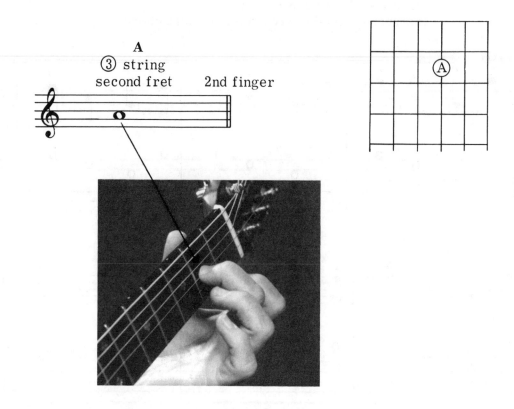

A
③ string
second fret   2nd finger

NOTES ON THE THIRD STRING

GABBY

THE NOTES ON THE FIRST THREE STRINGS
IN THE FIRST POSITION

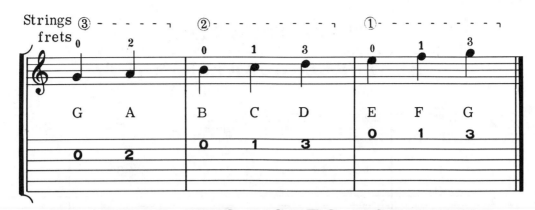

PLAYING TWO NOTES TOGETHER

When two or more notes are written on the same stem play them simultaneously as if they were one.

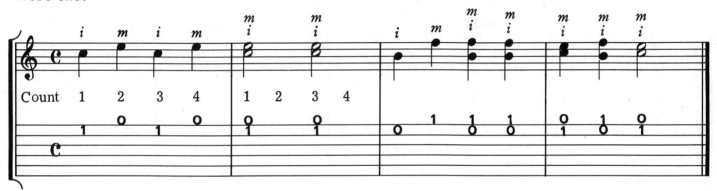

THE MONKEY SONG

DOTTED HALF NOTES

A dot placed after a note increases its value by one half. A dotted half note receives three beats or counts.

THREE FOUR TIME
In three four time, there are three counts per measure.

THE THREE QUARTER WALTZ

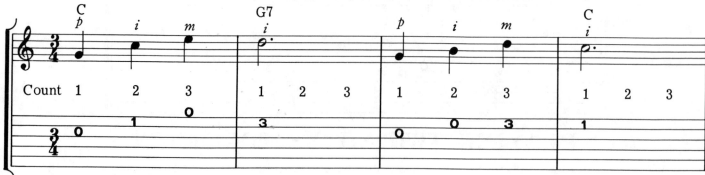

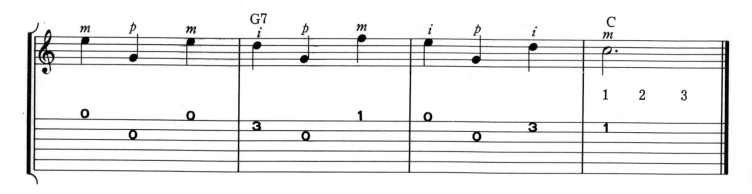

ONE AND TWO

When two notes are on the same stem play them simultaneously.

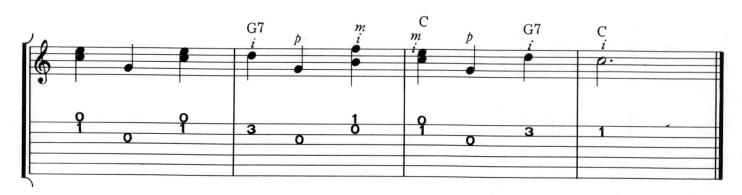

THE NOTES ON THE ④ STRING

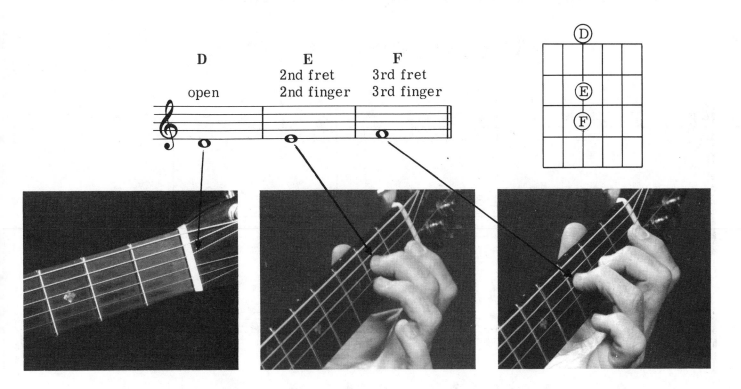

D	E	F
open	2nd fret	3rd fret
	2nd finger	3rd finger

THE NOTES ON THE ④ STRING

THE TWO STRING STROLL

REMEMBER When two notes are on the same stem play them as one.

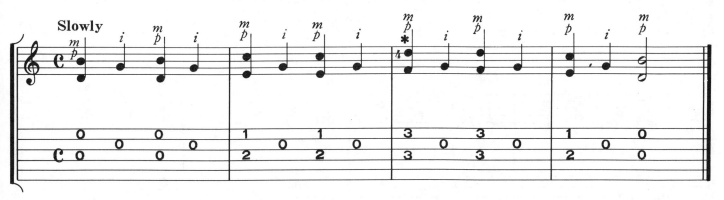

Slowly

* Use 4th finger on D note.

Practice the following solo using the *i* and *m* fingers.
When this is mastered, practice solo using the *p* and *i* picking.

THE ALTERNATE ROUTE

Tommy. Flint

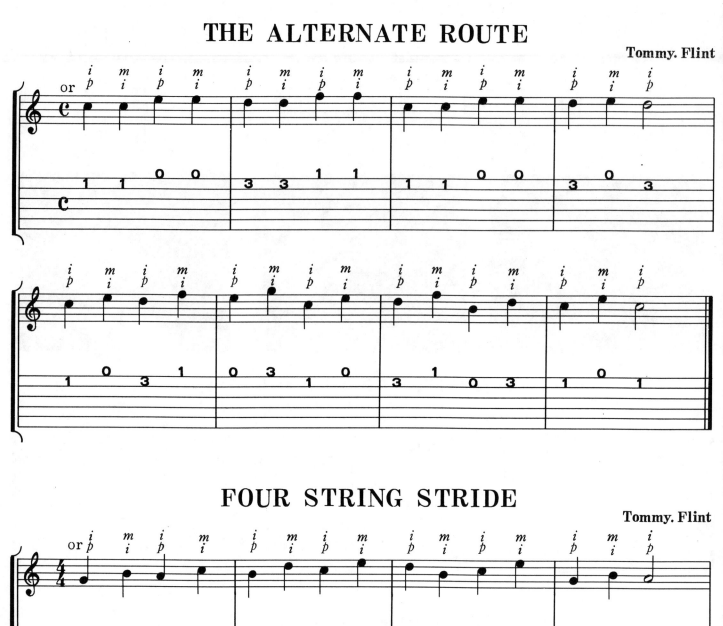

FOUR STRING STRIDE

Tommy. Flint

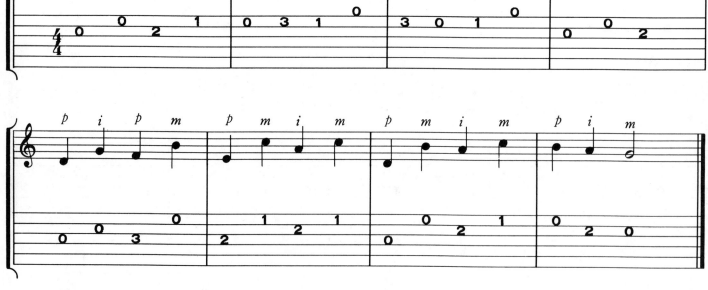

36

ROLL ALONG

Tommy Flint

WANDERING

Tommy Flint

* Use the third finger on "A" note.   * Play three strings simultaneously.
** Use the fourth finger on "D" note.   **

37

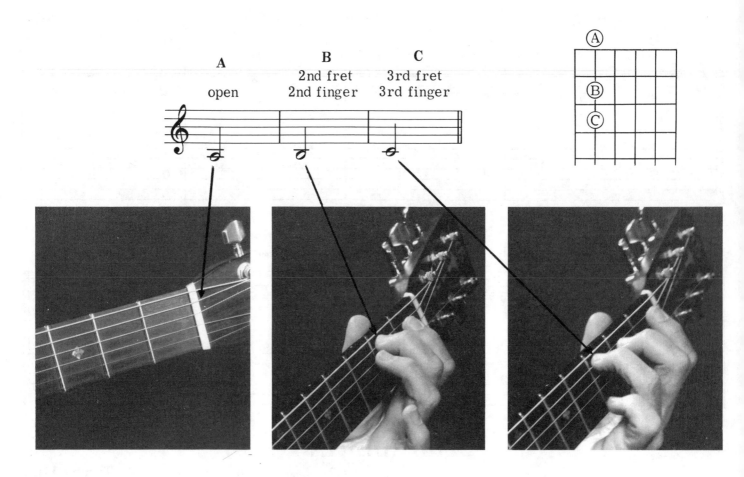

THE NOTES ON THE ⑤ STRING

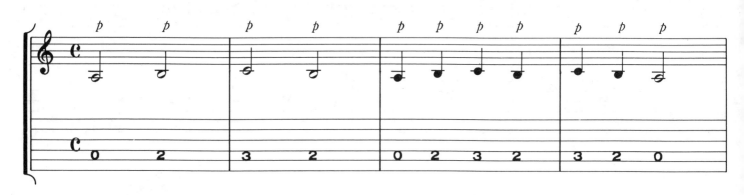

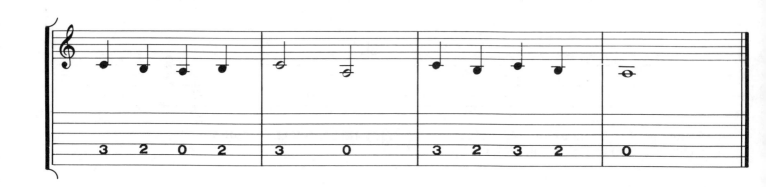

THUMBING

on the ⑤ and ④ strings

Tommy Flint

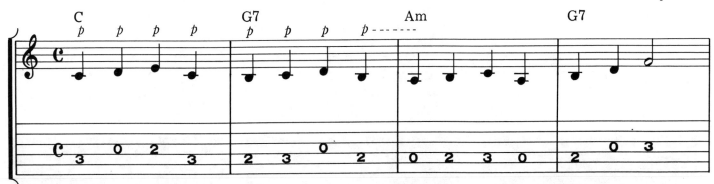

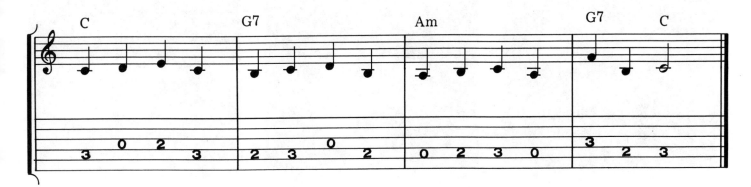

BACK AND FORTH

Practice both methods of picking.

Tommy Flint

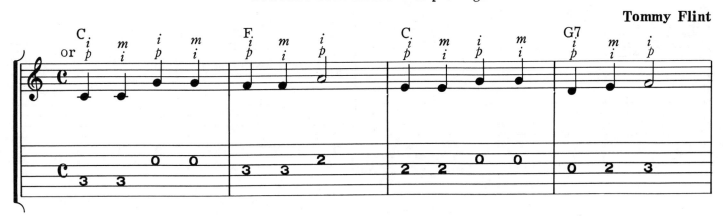

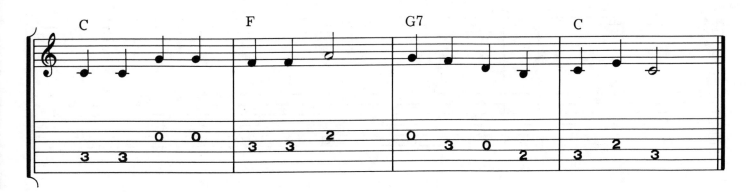

THE NOTES ON THE ⑥ STRING

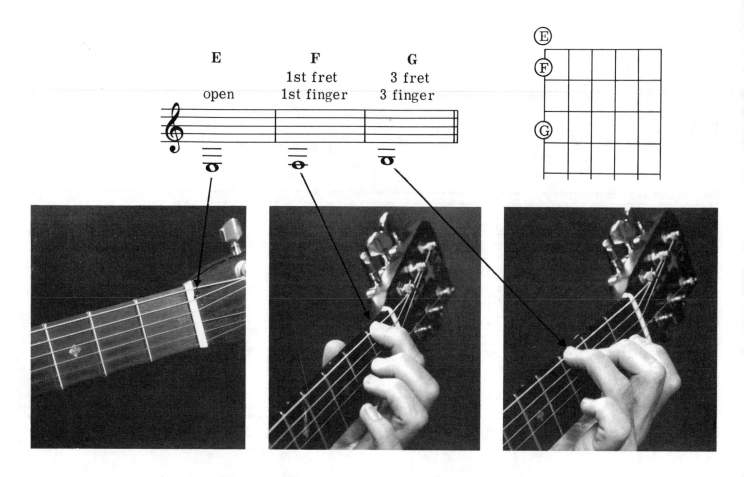

E	F	G
open	1st fret	3 fret
	1st finger	3 finger

THE NOTES ON THE ⑥ STRING

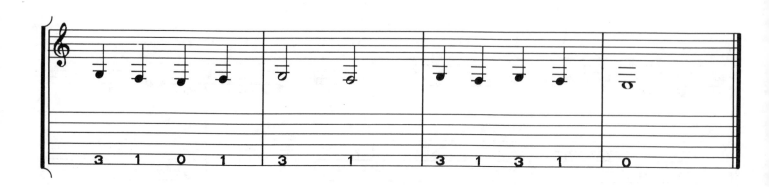

THUMPING THUMB

This sign means to repeat previous measure

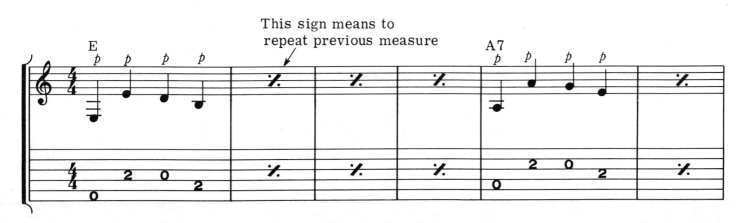

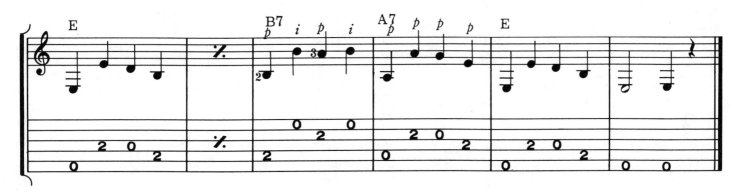

TWIDDLING

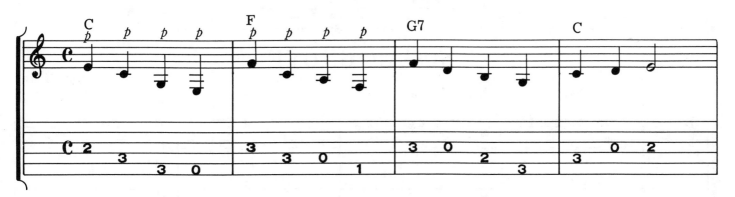

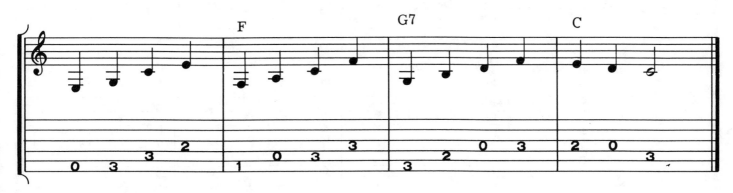

⁒ = Repeat previous measure.

MUSIC IN TWO PARTS

Generally speaking, when music is written in two parts, the notes with the stems turned downward will be plucked with the thumb.

The notes with the stems turned upward will be played with the fingers.

In the example at right the lower note is a dotted half and will be held or sustained for three beats.

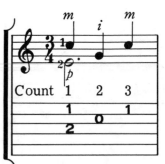

SAN MARINO WALTZ

Tommy Flint

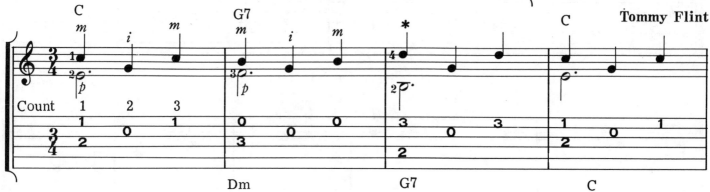

SUGAR GROVE

Tommy Flint

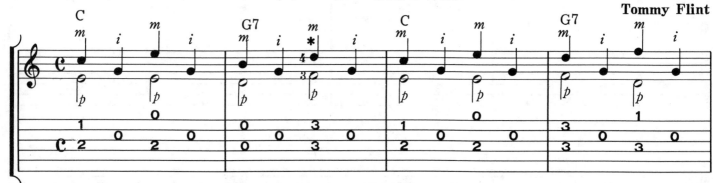

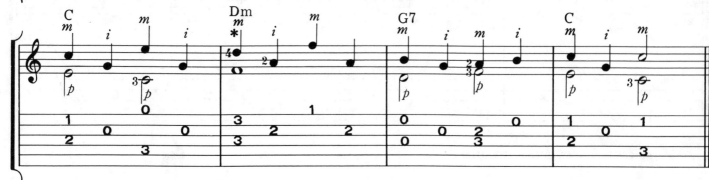

*Use fourth finger.

USING THE THIRD (a) FINGER

in the following solo the third finger will be used to pluck the ① string.

LONELY GUITAR
IN TWO PARTS

Tommy Flint

CEDAR RIDGE

Tommy Flint

* Fingers should remain on strings in order to sustain the tone.

"A" NOTE ON THE ① STRING

A
① string
5th fret 4 finger

THE BALTIC WALTZ

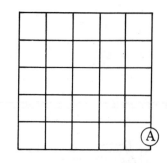

Tommy Flint

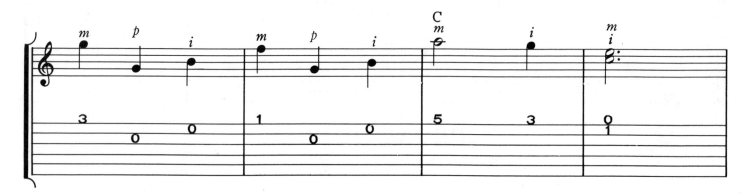

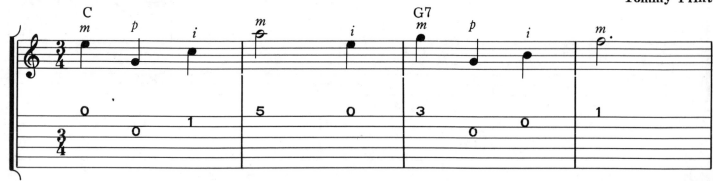

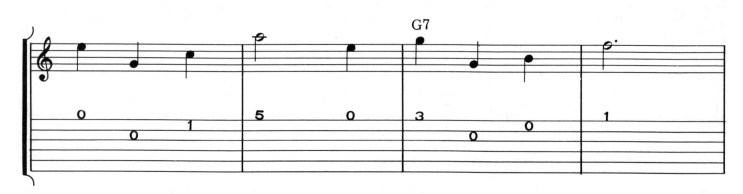

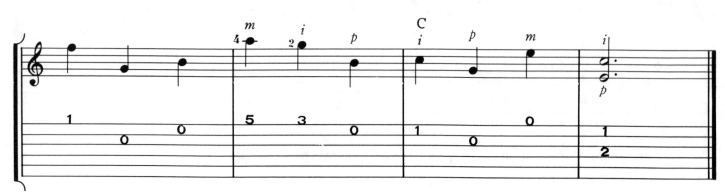

CHORDS

A chord consists of three or more notes played together.
In the example below, the notes in the first measure are played seperately.
In the second measure the notes are played simultaneously.

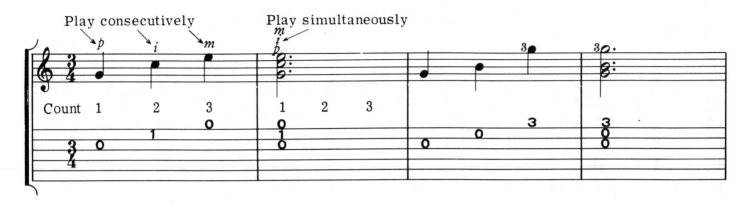

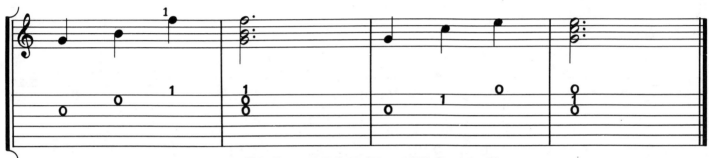

SOME MORE CHORDS

Reading chords is really no more difficult than reading single notes, due to the fact that each chord looks different because of the spacing of the notes on the staff, and can be recognized at a glance. Learn to recognize the chords without reading each note seperately.

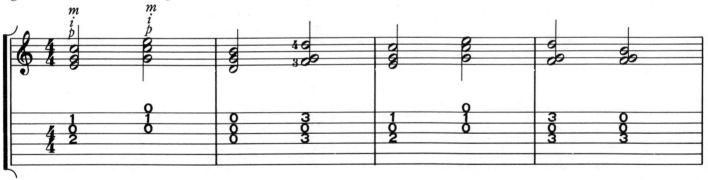

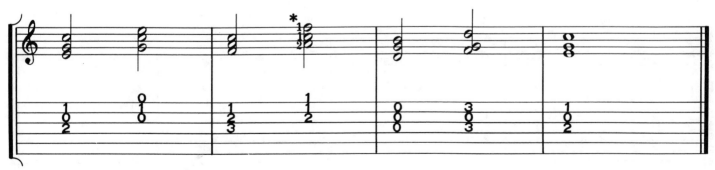

* Depress two strings (① and ②) with the first finger. Do <u>not</u> bend the finger at the first joint. The finger shoud lie flat on the fingerboard.

PICK UP NOTES

A song or melody does not always start on the count of one. If there are one or more notes at the beginning of a piece of music before the first measure, they are called pick up notes. Pick up notes are taken from the last measure.

In the solo below the pick up note is on the count of three.

THAT DOGGONE SONG

Note - The left hand fingering is very important in this tune.

* Use fourth finger.

A REVIEW OF THE NATURAL NOTES IN THE FIRST POSITION

The first finger determines the position. In other words, when playing in the first position, the first finger will be used to depress the string, or strings on the first fret. The second finger will be used to play any note located on the second fret, the third finger on the third fret and fourth finger will be used on the fourth fret.

Sometimes when making chords more than one finger will be located on the same fret.

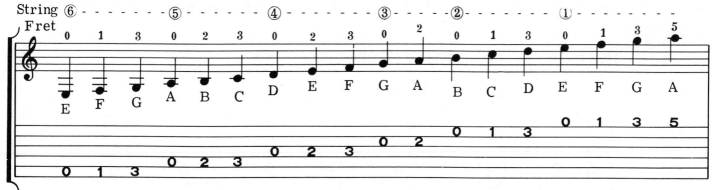

Play all notes and call the letter names aloud several times daily.

BALD MOUNTAIN

If you have trouble rembering any of the notes in the following solo, please refer to the above chart.

Moderate

Tommy Flint

47

THE KEY OF C

All music played so far in this book has been in the key of C. This means all notes have been in the C scale.

The C scale is a series of notes from C note to C an octave higher.

The distance between each note of the scale is a whole step, with the exception of the distance between the 3rd and 4th notes which is 1/2 step and the 7th and 8th notes which is 1/2 step. This is C MAJOR scale.

A <u>WHOLE STEP</u> is two frets on the guitar (from 1st to 3rd frets.)

A <u>1/2 STEP</u> is one fret on the guitar (from 1st to 2nd fret.)

THE C SCALE

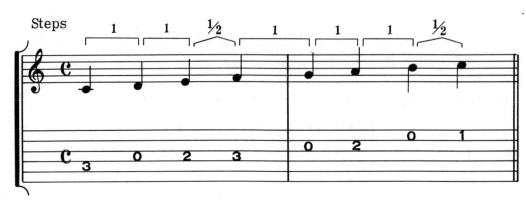

Please refer to page 19. The fingerboard and how to finger chords.

THE THREE PRINCIPAL CHORDS IN THE KEY OF C

The three principal chords are built on the 1st, 4th and 5th degrees or notes of the scale.
In other words the first note of the C scale is C, the fourth note of the scale is F and the fifth note of the scale is G. Therefore the chords are C, F and G7. or tonic, subdominant and dominant 7th.

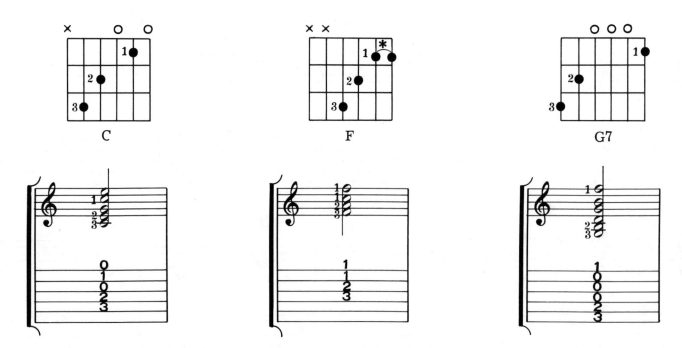

* Depress two strings with the same finger. Do not bend the finger at the first joint.

SINGLE NOTE MELODY WITH CHORD ACCOMPANIMENT, OR FILL IN

This style is written in two parts. The solo or melody will appear with the stems turned downward. The accompaniment or fill in will have the stems turned upward.

Unless otherwise indicated the THUMB will be used to play the melody notes and the FINGERS will be used to play the chords.

DAWSON WALTZ

Tommy Flint

49

ADDING NOTES TO THE CHORDS

In order to play all of the melody notes, it sometimes becomes necessary to add notes to the chords. In the chord diagrams below, the white circles on the strings show the notes that may be added by using the fourth and first fingers.

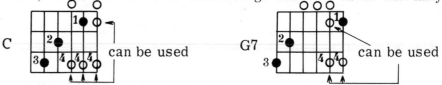

In the following solo the chord symbols are written above the music. This indicates that you hold the chord until you come to another symbol.

MEDLEY

The *m* and *i* fingers alternate throughout. The thumb plays the bass note.

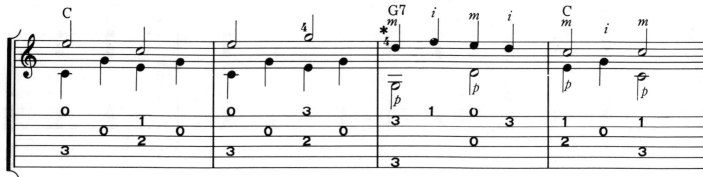

* Use fourth finger.

EIGHTH NOTES

The eighth note receives one half beat. Two eighth notes are equal to one quarter note. The eighth note has a flag on the stem. When two or more eighth notes are written in succession the stems may be connected by bars.

QUARTER NOTES

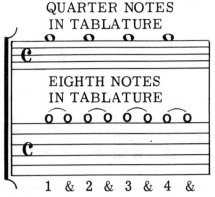

QUARTER NOTES
IN TABLATURE

EIGHTH NOTES IN TABLATURE

THE C SCALE IN EIGHTH NOTES

Practice slowly at first. Gradually increase tempo at each practice session.

AN EIGHTH NOTE EXERCISE ON THE C SCALE

Practice slowly at first

* Top row is suggested picking.

THINKING IN TERMS OF CHORDS

From this point on chord symbols will be written above the staff on some selections, even though the melody is in single notes. The student should begin thinking in terms of the chord that the melody notes are based on.

ROANOKE ROAD HOEDOWN

Tommy Flint

See Mel Bay's **E-Z WAY BLUEGRASS GUITAR SOLOS**

by Tommy Flint

CHROMATICS

 # SHARP The sharp sign placed before a note raises the pitch 1/2 step or one fret.

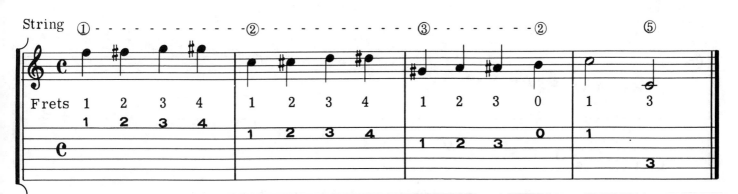

♭ FLAT The flat sign placed before a note lowers the pitch 1/2 step or one fret.

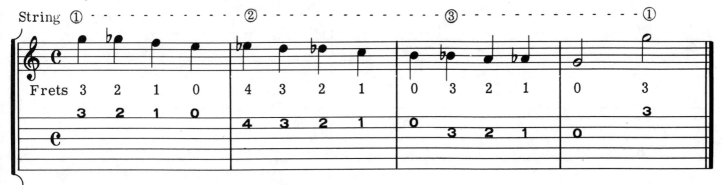

♮ NATURAL The natural sign cancels a sharp or flat. In other words, it restores a note to its normal position.

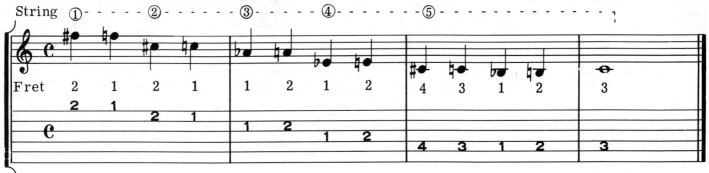

A BLUESY RUN

The accidental (#, ♭ , or ♮) is in effect for the duration of the measure.
The bar line will cancel the accidental.

NOTES IN THE FIRST POSITION

THE BLUES EVERY NIGHT

Slowly

Tommy Flint

A NEW CHORD

This chord is used in measure number nine.

B7

THE TIE

The tie is a curved line between two notes of the same pitch. The first note is played. The second note is not played but held and counted. Both notes are counted as if they were one.

THE SEAFARING MAN

Tommy Flint

THE DOTTED QUARTER NOTE

The dot after a note increases its value by one half. The dotted quarter note receives one and one half beats. The dotted quarter note is equal to three eighth notes.

In the following example the eighth note is played on the "&" half way between the counts of 2 and 3 and 4 and 1.

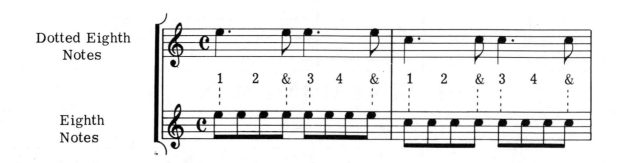

CLIMBING

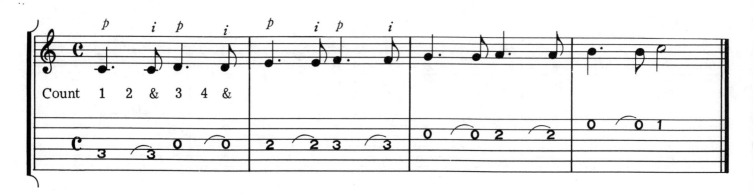

STEP BY STEP

Practice slowly and space the counts evenly.

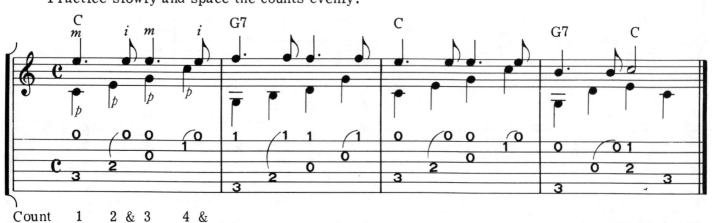

Count   1   2 & 3   4 &

MUSIC IN THREE PARTS

Occasionally, fingerstyle guitar music will be written in three parts.

In the example at right the first part or melody line has the stem turned upward. The second part or bass line has the stem turned downward.

The third part which is the rhythm or accompaniment also has the stems turned downward.

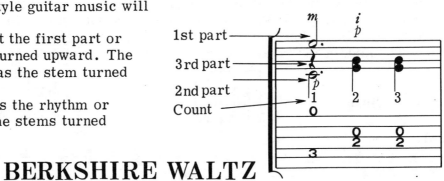

BERKSHIRE WALTZ

Tommy Flint

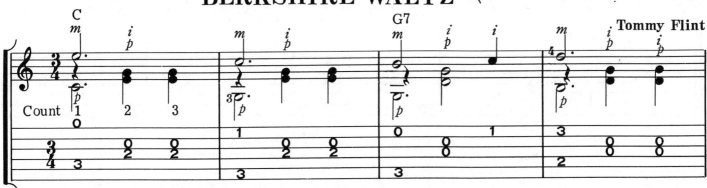

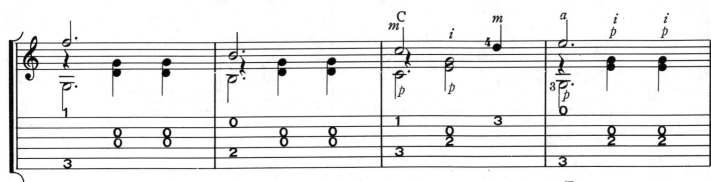

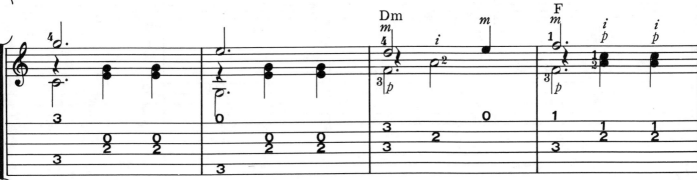

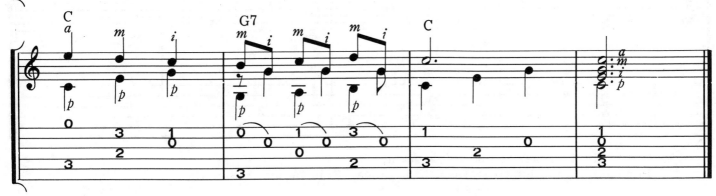

AMAZING GRACE

When playing in ¾ or waltz time the thumb and index finger are frequently used together to play the rhythm strokes. In measure number one of the following solo the thumb and middle finger are used on the first beat. The thumb and index finger are used to play the rhythm stroke on the second beat. The middle and index fingers are used for the eighth notes on the third beat.

rit. = Gradually decrease tempo. Slow down.

⌢ = Fermata. This sign indicates a long pause. Hold the note. Sustain.

MISTY RIDGE

Another solo using the new G7 chord (measures 4, 7 and 8.) and G13. All chord forms should be memorized as we will continue to use them throughout this book.

Tommy Flint

See Mel Bay's **"E-Z WAY FINGERSTYLE GUITAR SOLOS"**

by Tommy Flint

A NEW WAY TO PLAY B NOTE

The ③ string at the fourth fret is B note, the same as the ② string open.

When B is to be played on the ③ string it will be indicated by an encircled number above, below or beside the note.

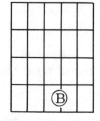

KEDGWICK

Tommy Flint

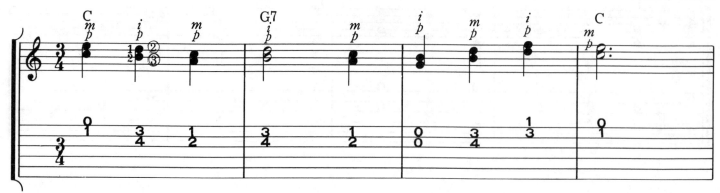

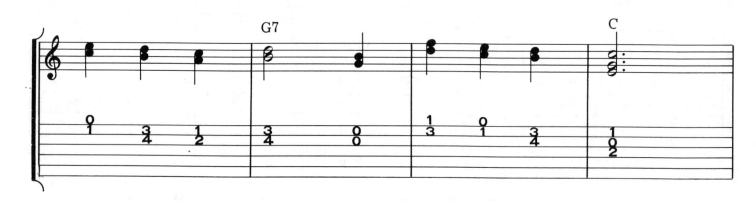

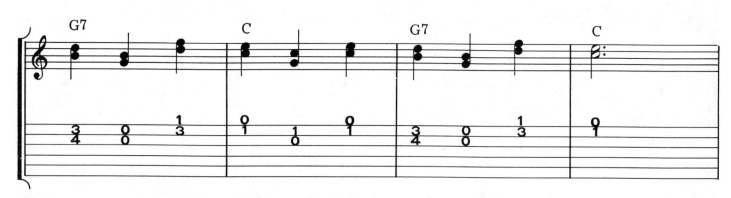

THE HALF BAR (BARRE)

To execute the half bar: The index finger should lay flat on the fingerboard, depressing the ①② and ③ strings. (Sometimes ④) Do not bend the finger at the first joint. (See photo) The thumb should remain on the back of the neck and the wrist should hang in a relaxed position. The palm of the hand should not touch the guitar neck.

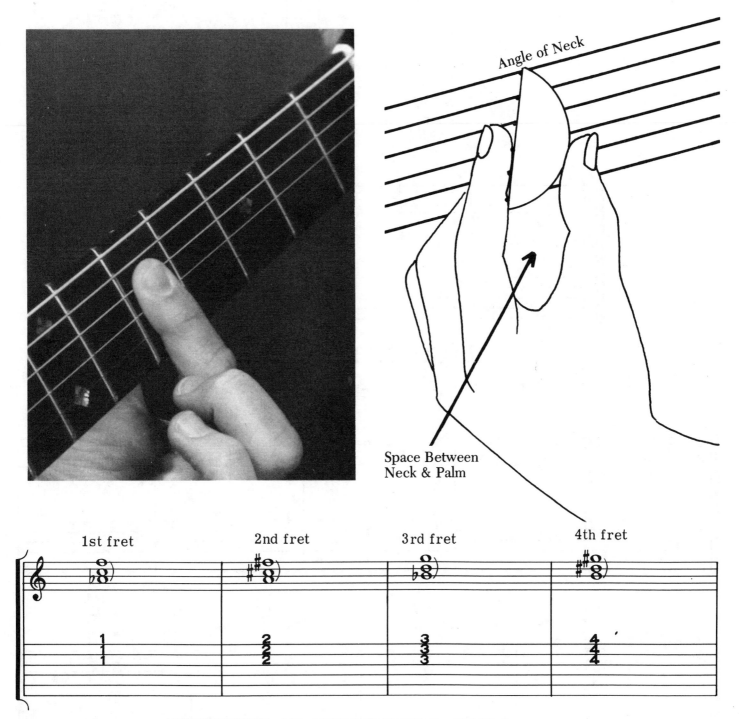

See Mel Bay's **ANTHOLOGY OF FINGERSTYLE GUITAR**

by Tommy Flint

THE NOTES ON ALL SIX STRINGS AT THE FIFTH FRET

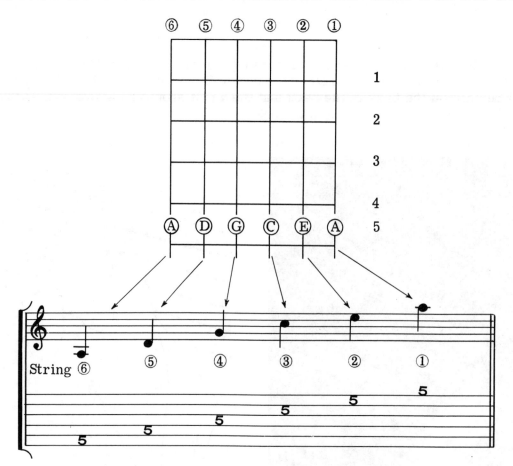

RACOON HOLLOW

Tommy Flint

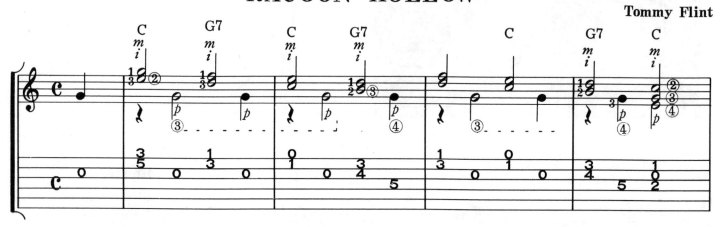

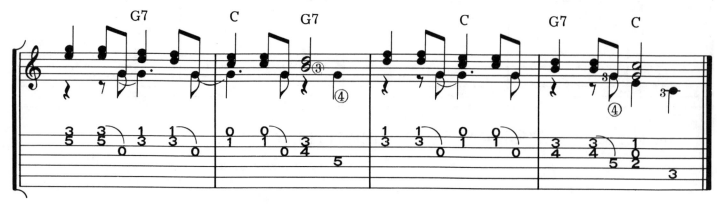

In the following solo the half bar is used at the fifth fret in measures 2, 7 and 10.

The chord diagram at right shows the fingering used in measures 3, 5 and 11.

Hold this chord in
measures 3, 5 and 11.

THE BALTIC WALTZ

Tommy Flint

Both fingers should remain in position in measures 3, 5 and 11.

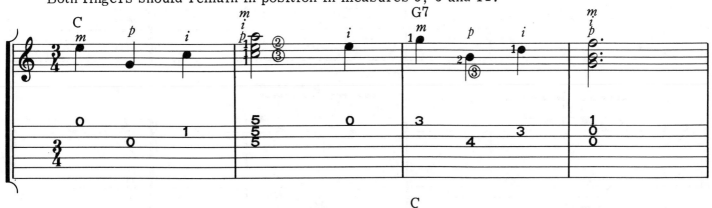

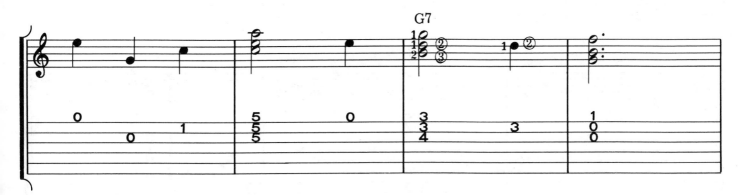

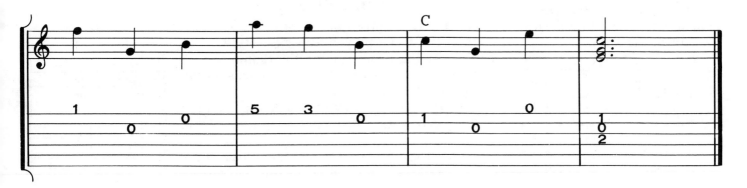

SOME RIGHT HAND EXERCISES

Practice each of the following until mastered.
Practice slowly at first gradually increasing the tempo with each practice session.

TWO NEW CHORDS

These chords will be used in the following solo.

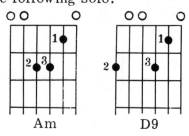

Am   D9

THE ARPEGGIO

A wavy line placed before a chord indicates that it is to be played arpeggio style.
To play the arpeggio use the thumb and roll over, or strum the notes consecutively from lowest to highest.
Or, the strings may be plucked p, i, m, a. This produces a beautiful harp like effect.

*The two dots before the double bar is a repeat sign. Repeat from the beginning.

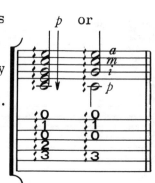

THE STREETS OF LAREDO
THREE VERSIONS

*While holding C chord lean the first finger over on the first string.

** While holding the chord lower the third joint section of the finger on the first string.

THE KEY OF A MINOR
RELATIVE TO C MAJOR

Every major key has a relative minor key.
The relative minor scale is built on the sixth tone of the major scale.
(The sixth tone of the C major scale is A)
The three most commonly used minor scales are:
    The 1 Natural   2 Harmonic   3 Melodic

THE A minor SCALES
NATURAL

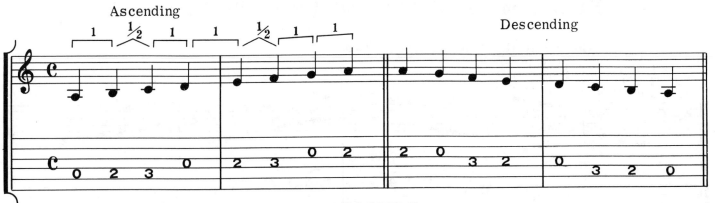

HARMONIC

The 7th tone is raised one half step both ascending and descending.
This is probably the most used of the minor scales.

MELODIC

The 6th and 7th tones are raised one half step on the ascending scale and lowered back to their normal pitch on the descending scale.

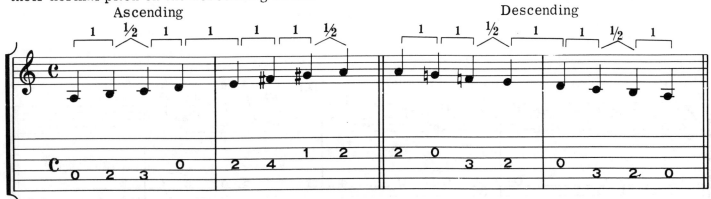

Memorize the three minor scales.

A NEW NOTE

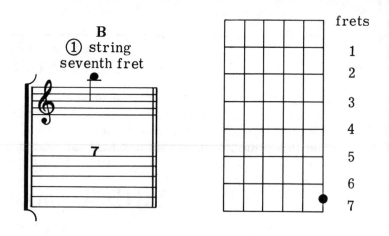

B
① string
seventh fret

THE A minor HARMONIC SCALE IN EIGHTH NOTES

Practice all three methods of picking.

A MINOR CLIMB

THE THREE PRINCIPAL CHORDS
KEY OF Am

The chords are built on the harmonic scale.

SOME ACCOMPANIMENT STYLES
No. 1

No. 2

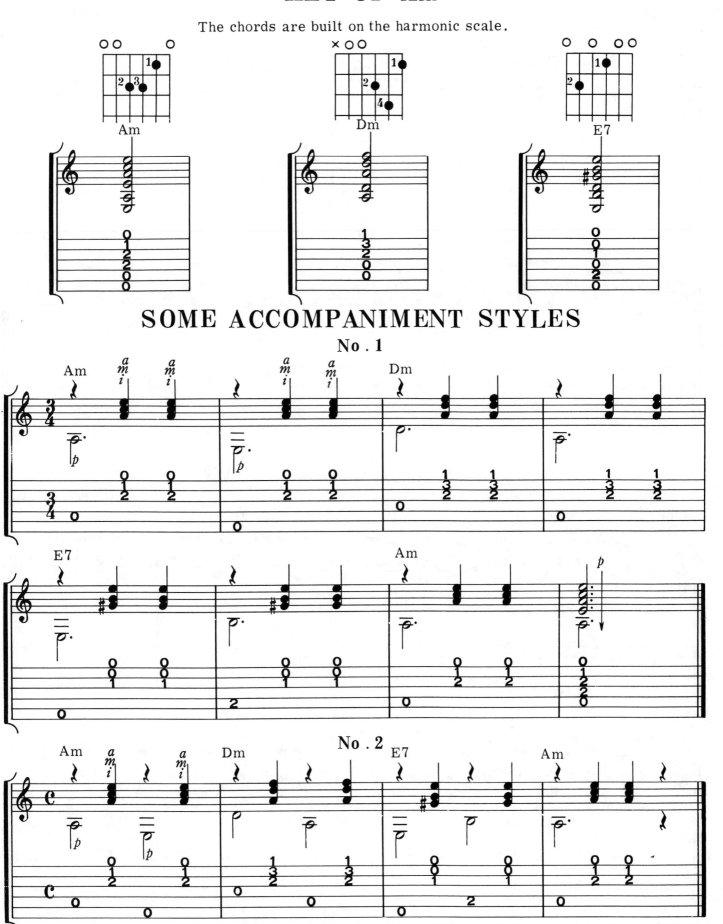

UKRAINIAN TUNE

Tommy Flint

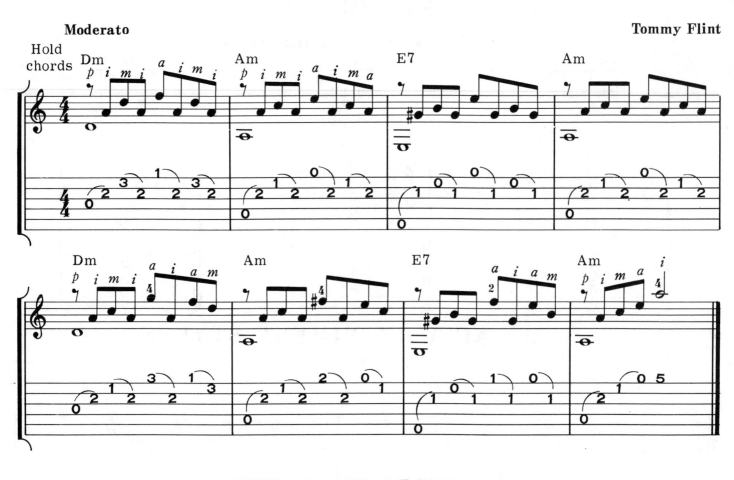

THE BLUE LIGURIAN

Tommy Flint

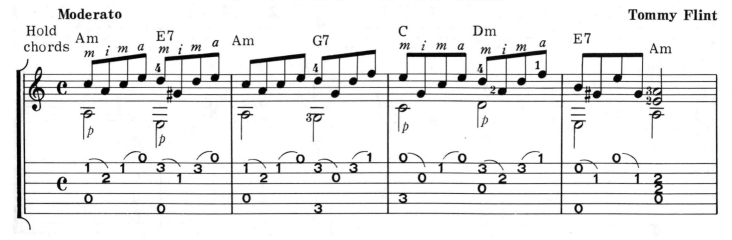

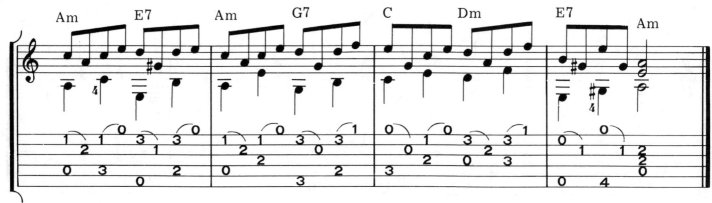

THE OPEN STRING CHORDS

Major Chords

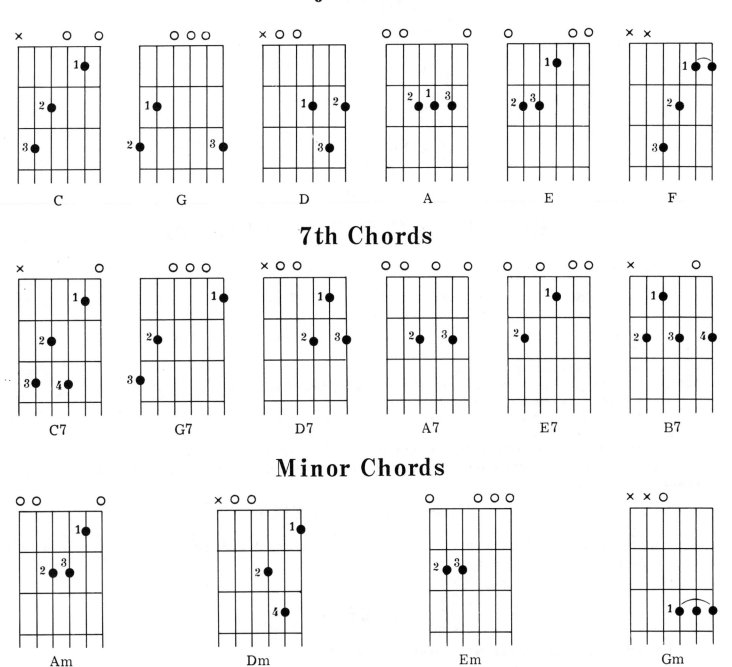

7th Chords

Minor Chords

I would suggest that you practice playing the three principal chords in the basic "Open String" keys. The principal chords are simply the three most commonly used chords in a given key. They just seem to fit together and sound very pleasant to the ear. Knowing how the chords fit together is an invaluable asset when playing by ear. It eliminates much of the guesswork and saves a great deal of time.

The three principal chords are called:

the TONIC, SUBDOMINANT and DOMINANT 7th

or the 1   4   and   5 Chords

It is very easy to find the three principal chords on the chord circle on the following page.

THE THREE PRINCIPAL CHORDS

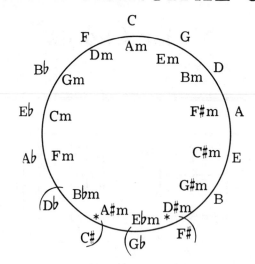

HOW TO FIND THE CHORDS

The three principal chords are:

TONIC   SUBDOMINANT   and   DOMINANT 7th
or   1   4   and   5

Pick out any chord on the circle. This is the tonic chord. Now move counterclockwise to the next chord.

This is the sub dominant chord.

The first chord clockwise to the tonic is the dominant 7th chord.

The dominant 7th naturally is a seventh chord.

As an example the chords in the key of C are C, F and G7.

In the key of G: G, C and D7 or the key of E: E, A and B7.

You now know enough chords to play in the keys of C, G, D, A and E.

The small letters inside the circle are the minor keys relative to the adjacent major keys outside the circle.

HOW TO PRACTICE

Play the tonic, sub dom. dom. 7th and tonic. Use the thumb and strum each chord four beats spacing the counts as evenly as a clock.

EXAMPLE

Each diagonal line represents a strum with the thumb.

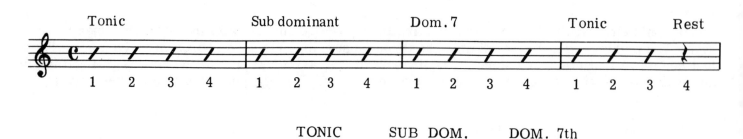

The principal chord may be

	TONIC	SUB DOM.	DOM. 7th
	Maj.	Maj.	7th
or	mi	mi	7th

* The fingering for D♭ and C♯ is identical. Also G♭ and F♯ are identical.

THE CASCADE RANGE

Tommy Flint

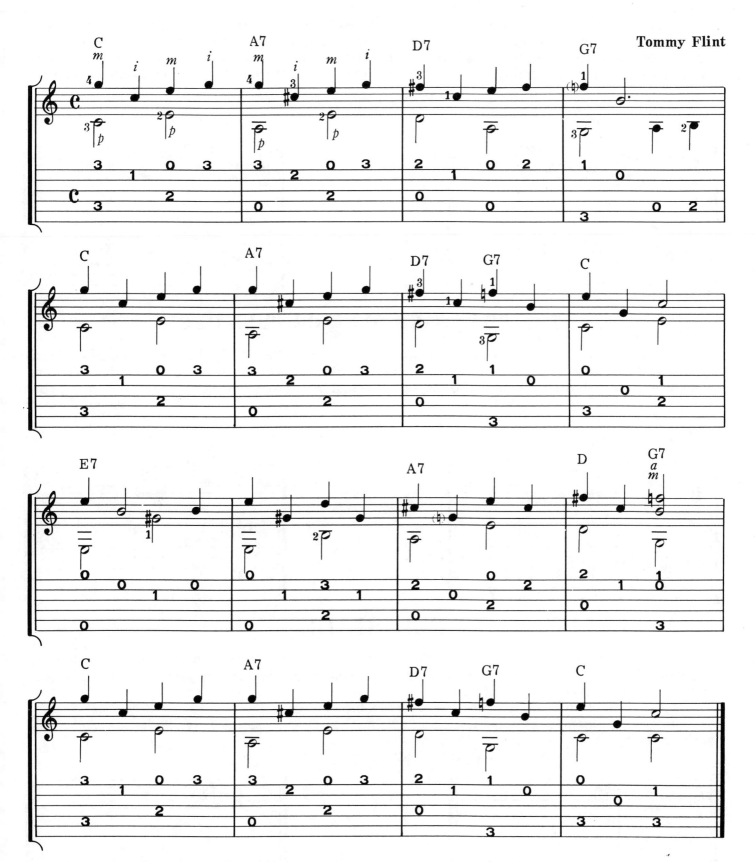

See Mel Bay's **E-Z GUITAR BLUES SOLOS**
by Tommy Flint

SLURS
THE UPWARD SLUR OR HAMMER ON

The upward slur or hammer on will be indicated by a curved line. To hammer on, pluck an open string and while the string is still ringing hammer (press down abruptly) the left hand finger on the correct note. It is also possible to hold a string down at any fret and using a different left hand finger hammer the string on a higher fret. Pick the first note. Do not pick the second note.

EXAMPLE

Open

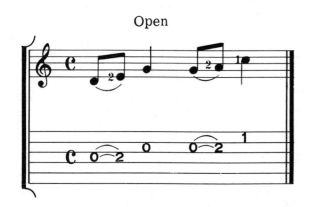

Closed

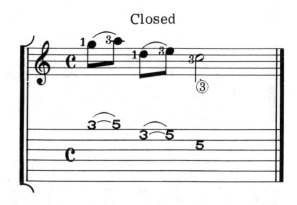

THE DOWNWARD SLUR OR PULL OFF

The downward slur or pull off is the opposite of hammering on. Strike the higher note. Then while it is still ringing pull the finger off, thus allowing the lower note to sound. Do not just lift the finger, but pull off at an angle (to the side). Actually the finger plucks the string as it is pulled off.

Open

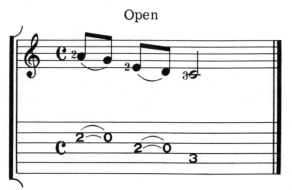

Closed

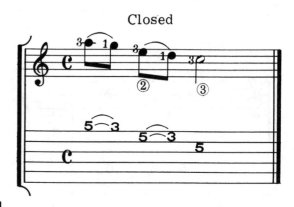

THE SLIDE

To slide into a note or chord place the fingers one or more frets below the note you intend to play. Immediately after striking the note or chord slide up to the correct position, while keeping the fingers depressed on the strings.

Pick the first note. Do not pick the second note, slide into it.

In the first example pick the C note on the "and" after the count of four. Slide into the C♯ note on the count of one.

In the second example slide on the count of one.

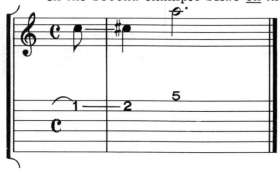

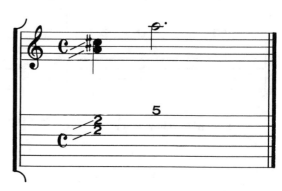

WILDWOOD FLOWER

KEY SIGNATURES

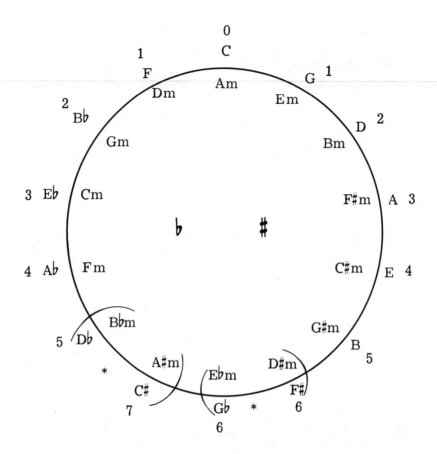

Starting at the top of the circle and moving clockwise, gives the sharp keys. Starting at the top of the circle and moving counterclockwise gives the flat keys. Every major key has a relative minor key, which is written in the same key signature. As an example the key of G has one sharp. The relative minor key of E minor also has one sharp. (The relative minor keys are on the inside of the circle.) The key of C has no sharps or flats A minor is the relative minor key. The Arabic numeral beside the letter indicates the number of sharps or flats in the key signature.

Ther are seven natural notes in the musical alphabet: A B C D E F and G. Between the natural notes are the sharps (♯) and flats (♭).

As we move clockwise around the circle the keys or chords move in fifths, or in other words, five notes on the musical alphabet. Example C D E F G.
or 1 2 3 4 5.

As we move counterclockwise on the circle the keys or chords move in fourths. Example:
C D E F.
or 1 2 3 4.

When we start with C and move counterclockwise through the flat keys, each time we move one key one flat is added to the key signature. The key of F has one flat, B♭ has two flats, E♭ has three flats etc.

As we start with C and move clockwise through the sharp keys, each time we move one key a sharp is added to the key signature. The key of G has one sharp, the key of D has two sharps, the key of A has three sharps etc.

KEY SIGNATURES

See Mel Bay's **THEORY & HARMONY FOR EVERYONE**

by L. Dean Bye

CHINQUAPIN

Tommy Flint

LIBERTY

An exercise in single string picking. Practice slowly at first. Gradually increase the tempo with each practice session.

See Mel Bay's **LEARN TO PLAY BLUEGRASS GUITAR**

by Tommy Flint

THE KEY OF G

The key of G has one sharp in the key signature. The sharp sign is on the F line. This indicates that all F notes will be played as F♯, or one fret higher.

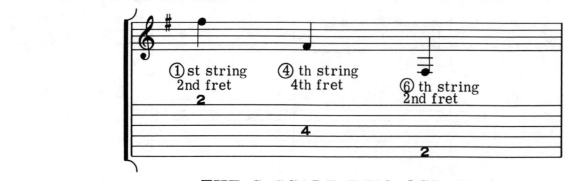

THE G SCALE TWO OCTAVES

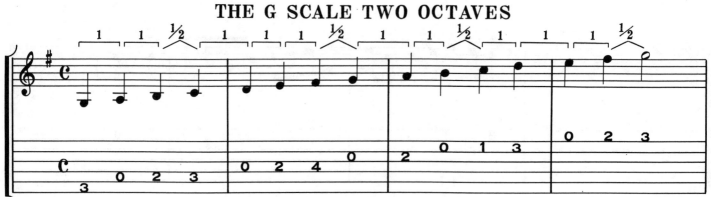

THE THREE PRINCIPAL CHORDS IN THE
KEY OF G

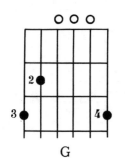

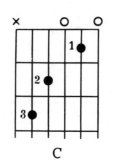

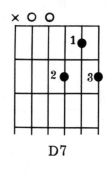

COUNTRY RHYTHM IN THE KEY OF G

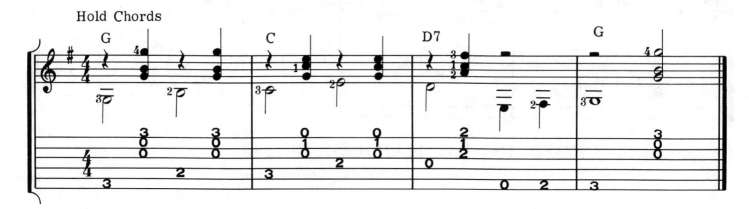

JANESVILLE WALTZ

Tommy Flint

*Refer to page 62. Notes on the fifth fret on all six strings.

81

GENOA HOLIDAY

Moderate Waltz

Tommy Flint

Notice that the fourth finger is used on the ② string when playing G chord except in measures 10 and 16. This is necessary in order to play the melody notes.

THE KEY OF E MINOR
RELATIVE TO G MAJOR

The key of E minor has one sharp in the key signature.

THE HARMONIC SCALE
TWO OCTAVES
Ascending

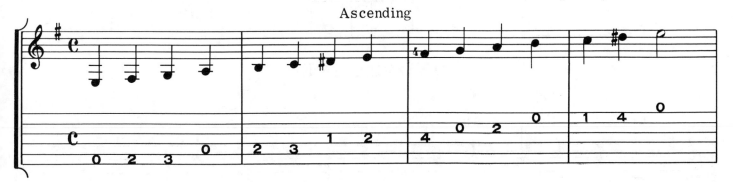

Descending

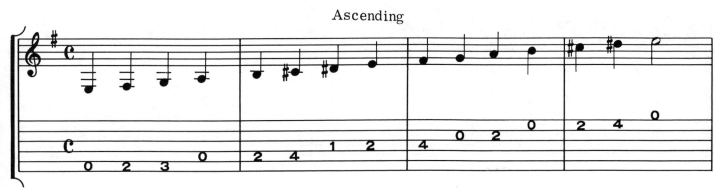

THE MELODIC SCALE
TWO OCTAVES
Ascending

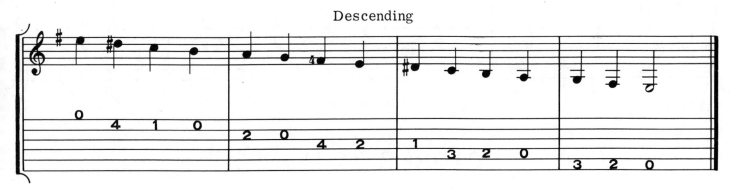

Descending

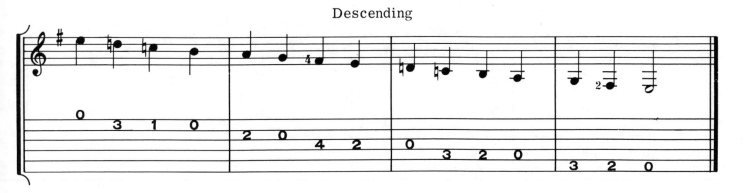

THE THREE PRINCIPAL CHORDS IN THE KEY OF E minor

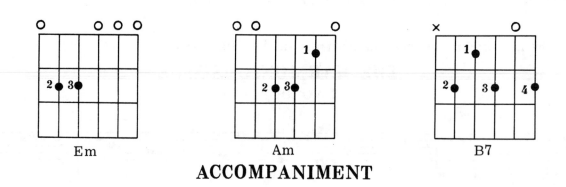

ACCOMPANIMENT

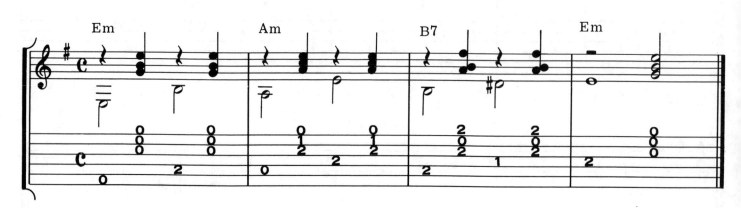

OCTOBER TWILIGHT

Moderately slow

Tommy Flint

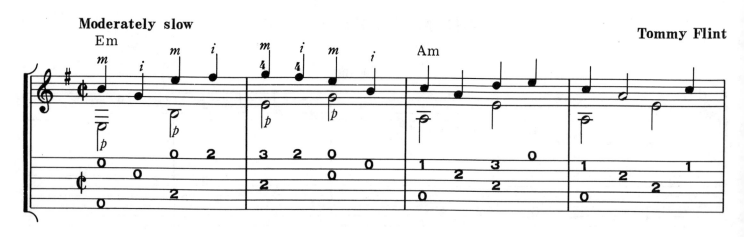

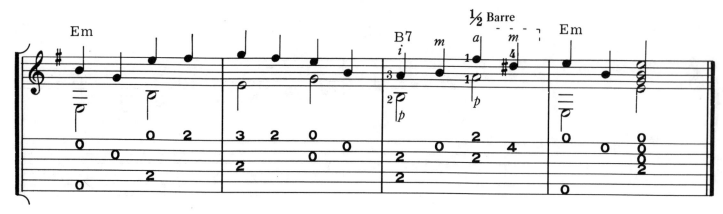

THE PAINTED HILLS

Moderate

Tommy Flint

can be
used ⟶ A9

ETUDE

Hold chords

Tommy Flint

*If it is too difficult to play C note while holding Am chord, E note on the ④ string may be substituted.

When changing from D7 to G chord the fingering shown at right is preferred. When changing from C to G use original fingering.

ALPINE WALTZ

Tommy Flint

LULLABYE

Johann Brahms
Arr. By Tommy Flint

See Mel Bay's **ANTHOLOGY OF FINGERSTYLE GUITER**

by **Tommy Flint**

BEECH TREE LANE

Tommy Flint

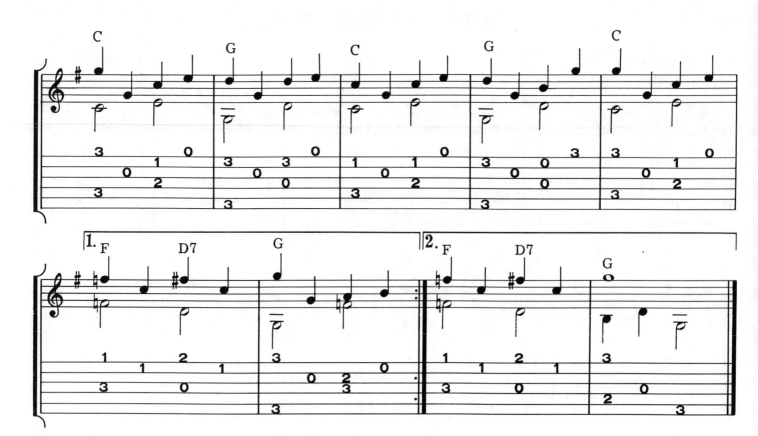

TWO FOUR TIME

Two four time has two beats per measure.
The quarter note receives one beat.

Beats — Quarter note

UP AND DOWN

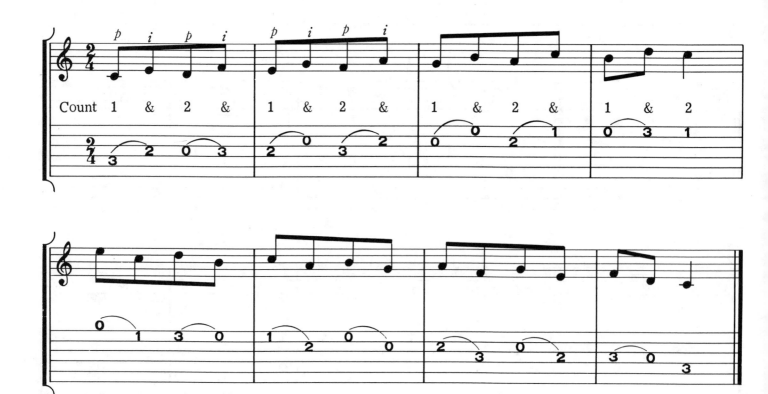

Count 1 & 2 & | 1 & 2 & | 1 & 2 & | 1 & 2

VINEYARDS ON THE RHINE

Practice slowly at first. Gradually increase tempo with each practice session.

Tommy Flint

*See page 62.

RIGHT HAND DEVELOPMENT

No.1

Hold chords. Practice slowly at first.

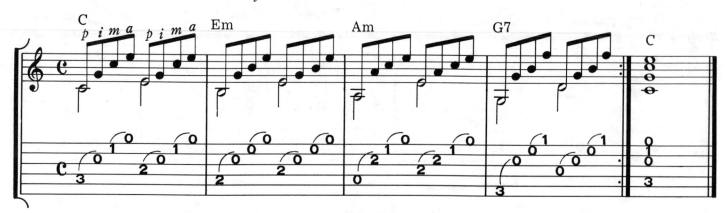

No.2

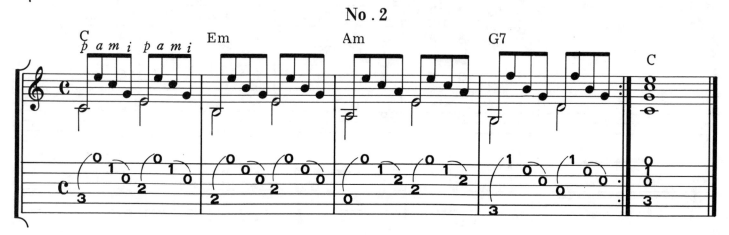

No.3

No.4

No. 5

The three following exercises are excellent styles to use as background or rhythm patterns to accompany a vocalist or lead instrument.

No. 6

No. 7

No. 8

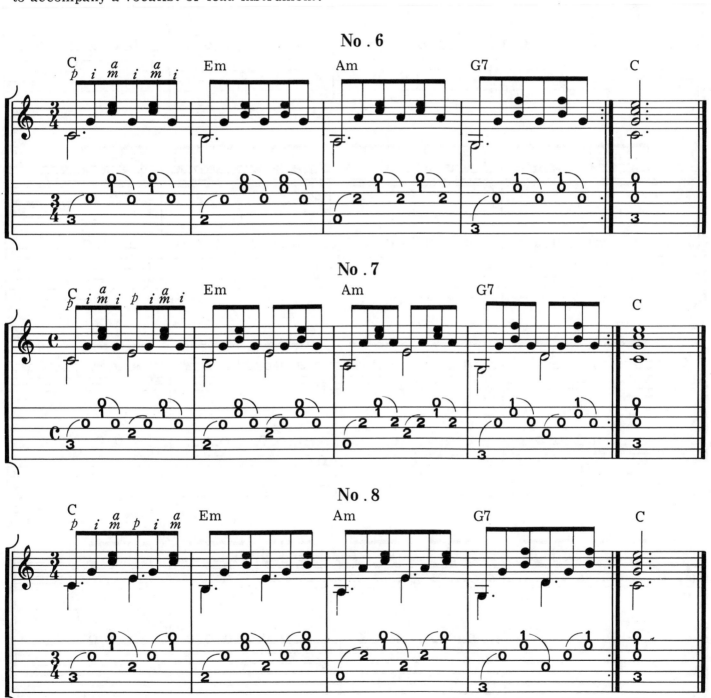

A RIGHT HAND DEVELOPMENT EXERCISE
USING THE Am AND C SCALES

Practice the following exercise using each of the picking patterns shown below.

1. *p i m a*		4. *p m i m*
2. *p a m i*		5. *p m a m*
3. *p i m i*		6. *p a m a*

This exercise should be practiced daily. Practice slowly at first gradually increasing the speed with each practice session.

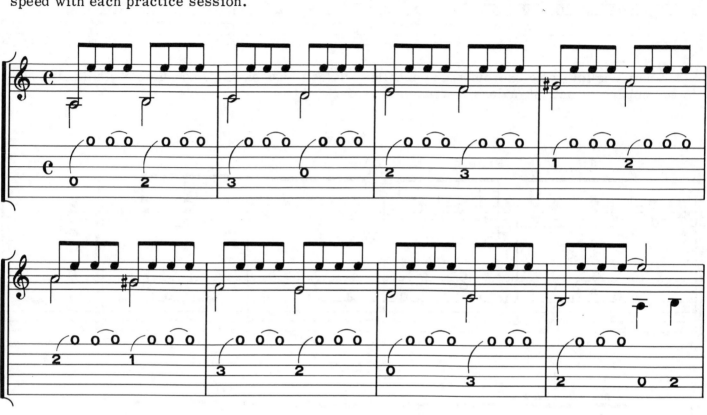

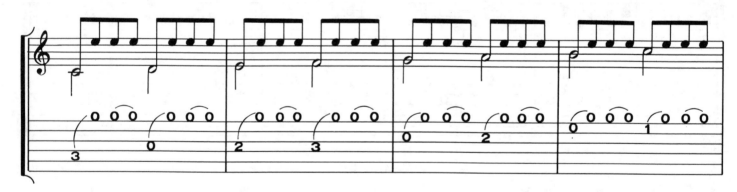

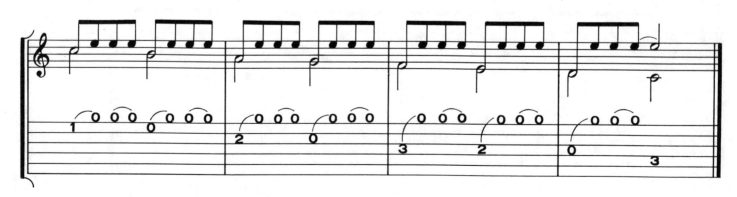

HOTFOOT

Use *p* ^m_i then *p* ^a_m

Tommy Flint

95

ALLA-BREVE TIME

ALLA-BREVE TIME is commonly referred to as CUT TIME.
The alla-breve time signature has a vertical line draw through the letter C.
Alla-breve time has two counts per measure.
When a melody is to be played in a fast tempo, it is sometimes easier to count two beats per measure rather than four. This is especially true of hoe downs, fiddle tunes and sixteenth notes.

ALLA - BREVE TIME

CRIPPLE CREEK

See Mel Bay's **100 E-Z WAY FLATPICKING GUITAR SOLOS**

by Tommy Flint

ON GEORGIAN BAY

Tommy Flint

A NEW NOTE

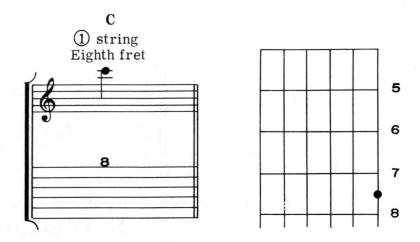

C
① string
Eighth fret

AN EXERCISE ON THE ① STRING

F AND G NOTES ON THE ② STRING

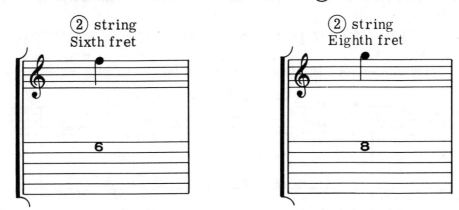

② string
Sixth fret

② string
Eighth fret

AN EXERCISE ON THE ② STRING

D NOTE ON THE ③ STRING

③ string
seventh fret

C SCALE ON THE ③ ② AND ① STRINGS
FIFTH POSITION

The first finger determines the position. When your first finger is on the first fret, you are in the first position. When your first finger is on the fifth fret, you are in the fifth position. The other fingers are placed accordingly. The positions will be covered more thouroughly later on.

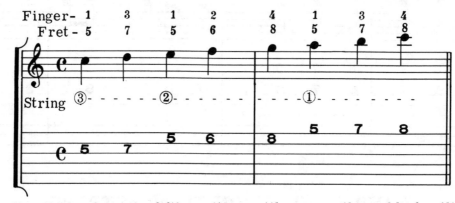

Practice reading the scale in the fifth position until you are thourghly familiar with the notes and have memorized the fingering.

A SCALE EXERCISE IN THE FIFTH POSITION

Practice very slowly at first, gradually increasing the tempo with each session.
In the fifth measure on the second count use the half bar when playing E and C.

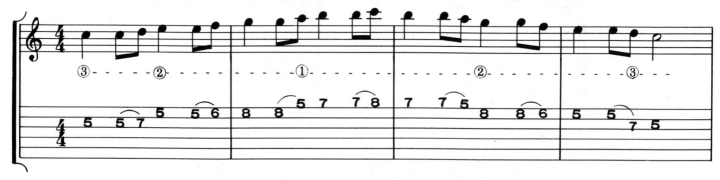

THE NORTH BAY WALTZ

The first eight measures are in the fifth position with the exception of the open G string. measures nine through sixteen span the fingerboard from the first to the eighth fret.

Use the half bar in measures 2, 6, 10, and 11.

Tommy Flint

PRELUDE
PLAY LEGATO (HOLD CHORDS)

Use half bar in measures 1, 4, 5, 8, 9, 12, 13 and 16.

Tommy Flint

LEGATO

The term legato means to play smoothly as if the notes are connected. Let one note flow into the next.

A curved line over a passage of notes indicates that they are to be played legato. If possible, hold the chord.

The legato sign

③ string
Ninth fret

IMPORTANT

The fingering to the following chords should be memorized as the same forms will be used over and over again in playing solos in various keys.

C SCALE (HARMONIZED)

Play slowly

A MINOR SCALE (HARMONIZED)

Play slowly

half bar

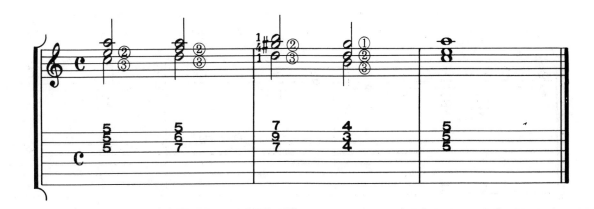

G SCALE (HARMONIZED)

Play slowly

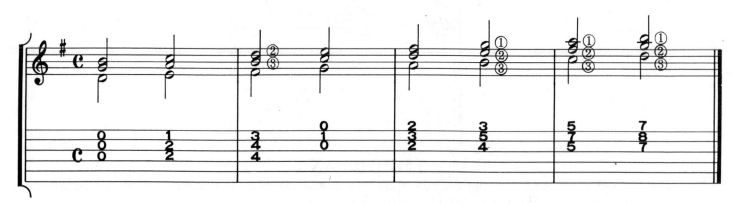

E MINOR SCALE (HARMONIZED)

Play slowly

PLAY THE FOLLOWING EXERCISES LEGATO

A Minor

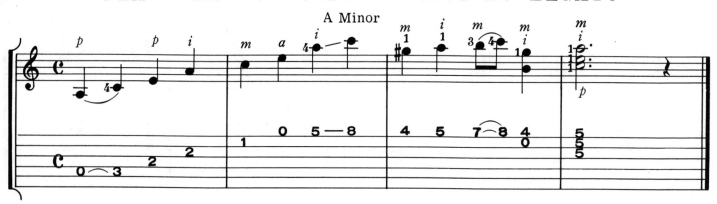

E Minor

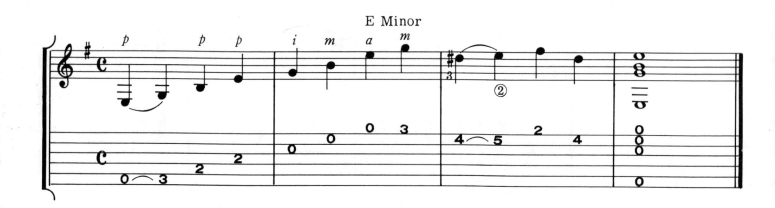

LEGEND OF THE CARPATHIANS

Tommy Flint

TRIPLETS

The term triplet indicates a group of <u>three</u> notes played in the time of <u>two</u> notes of the same kind. The triplets will usually be indicated by the number three and a bracket above or below the stems.

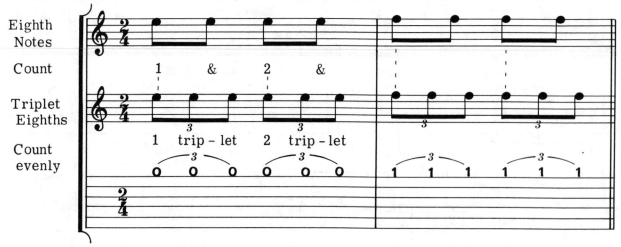

TRIPLETS ON THE C SCALE

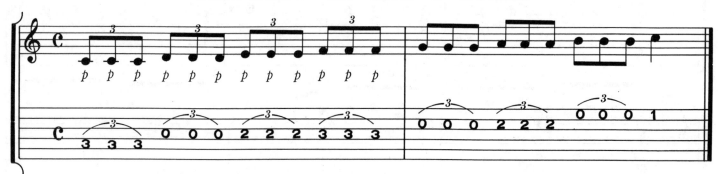

SOME PICKING EXERCISES IN TRIPLETS

Practice the following exercise using *p i m*, then *p m a*!
Practice slowly

No. 1

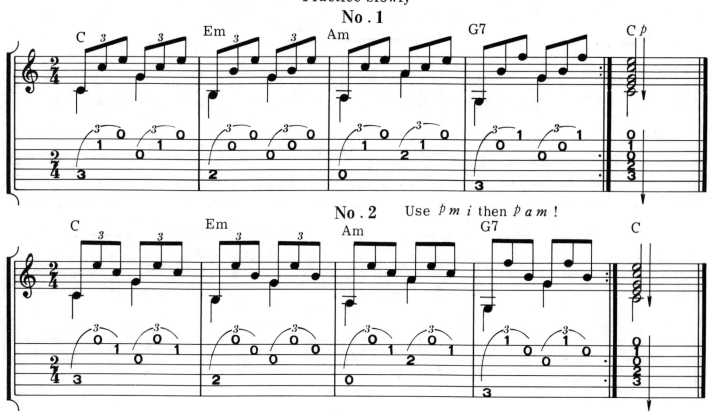

No. 2   Use *p m i* then *p a m*!

106

RIGHT HAND DEVELOPMENT USING TRIPLETS

Use 1. *p i m* 2. *p m a* 3. *p m i* 4. *p a m* 5. *p i a* 6. *p a i*

Practice slowly at first

EAGLE PASS

Tommy Flint

SINGLE STRING TRIPLETS

When triplets are played on a single string, alternate picking is used. However the picking is reversed on each group of notes, due to the three notes in each group.

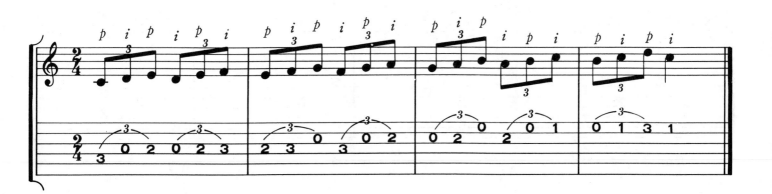

THE MERRYMAKER

Tommy Flint

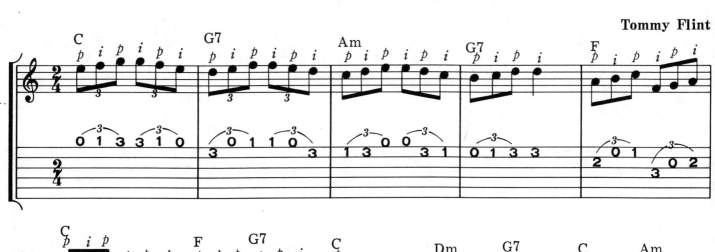

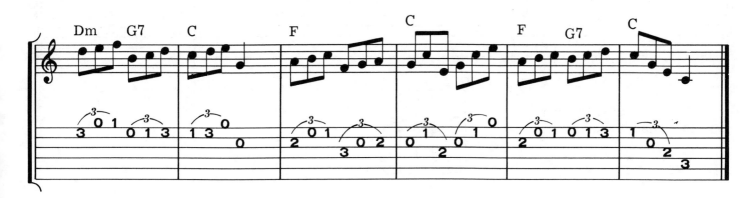

THE NORTH PLATTE

Moderate

Tommy Flint

This A7 chord is used
in measure 4 and 12.

A7

A THUMB EXERCISE
Hold Chords
All notes are plucked with the thumb.

Rest the fourth finger (right hand) on the pick guard or guitar top.

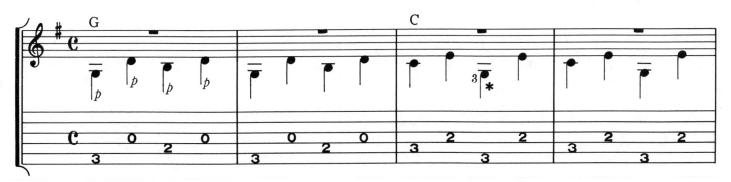

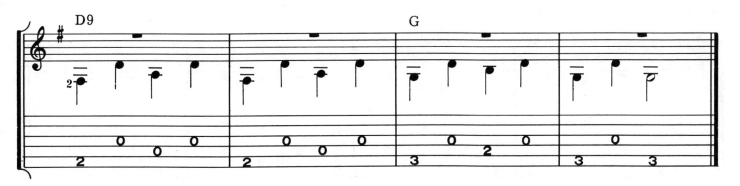

In the following exercise the thumb continues to play the steady bass line while the index finger plays the melody line.

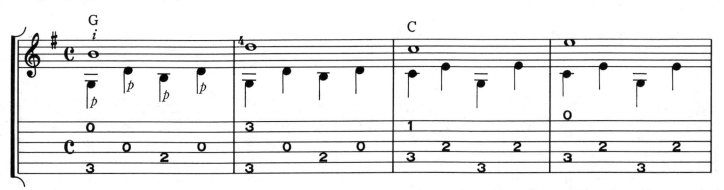

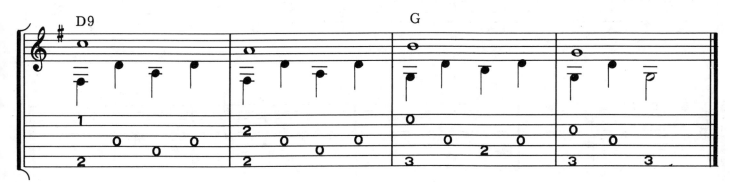

* While holding C chord move the third finger to G note on the ⑥ string to play the bass note.

MELODY on one and three with a steady bass.

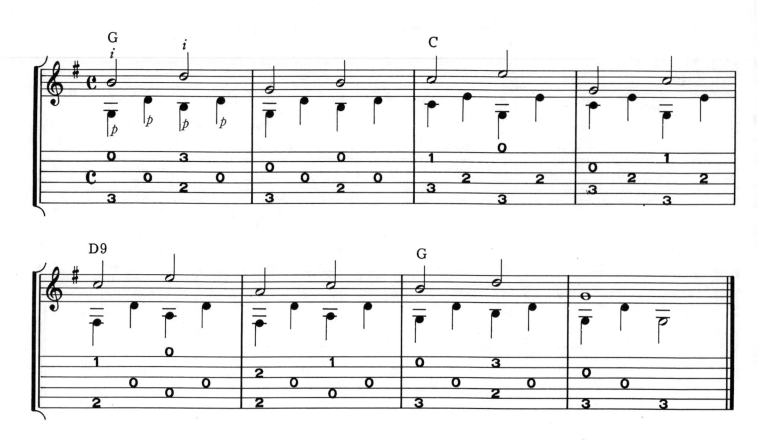

MELODY on one three and four with steady bass.

THUMB AND FINGER STYLE
SOMETIMES REFERRED TO AS
TRAVIS PICKING

Various terms have been used to describe this style such as "THUMB STYLE", "FINGER STYLE", " THUMP BASS" "CLAW HAMMER" and "HOG WALLOW PICKIN" to name a few. but probably the most commonly used term today is "TRAVIS PICKIN".

It was the legendary MERLE TRAVIS who learned this style from MOSE RAGER and IKE EVERLY and then developed it to a high degree of complexity and introduced it to the world by way of radio, records and T.V.

In this style two or more parts are played simultaneously on one guitar. The thumb plays rhythm on the bass strings and lower part of the chord while the fingers play the melody or syncopated improvisation on the treble strings and upper part of the chord. The bass strings are muffled by the heel of the hand.

HOW TO MUFFLE THE BASS STRINGS

The heel of the right hand should muffle the three bass strings near the bridge in order to produce a muted, solid thump tone. Do not touch the strings too far away from the bridge or you will get a dead thud. If you touch them too close to the bridge they will ring too much. It will take a bit of practice and experimentation to find the right sound.

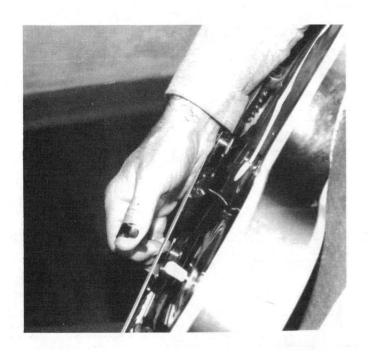 

HOW TO MUFFLE THE STRINGS

See page 68 in Mel Bay's ANTHOLOGY OF FINGERSTYLE GUITAR
by Tommy Flint

SOUTHERN STYLE

See Mel Bay's **MERLE TRAVIS GUITAR STYLE**

by **Merle Travis and Tommy Flint**

THUMBSTYLE FESTIVAL

Tommy Flint

D.C. al Fine - Back to the beginning
and play to Fine

* On the first beat the first finger is on A note on
the ③ string. On the third beat the first finger
is on B note on the ⑤ string.

SYNCOPATION

A very colorful and outstanding ingredient of this style is the flowing, spontaneous feel of the melody above the steady muffled bass rhythm. This is achieved by syncopation. The definition of syncopation is "irregularity of rhythm" or placing the accents on beats which are usually unaccented. In this section syncopation means that the melody notes are sometimes played between the rhythm beats of the thumb.

NO.1

The melody notes are played on "&" after the first and second beats, halfway between the rhythm beats of the thumb.

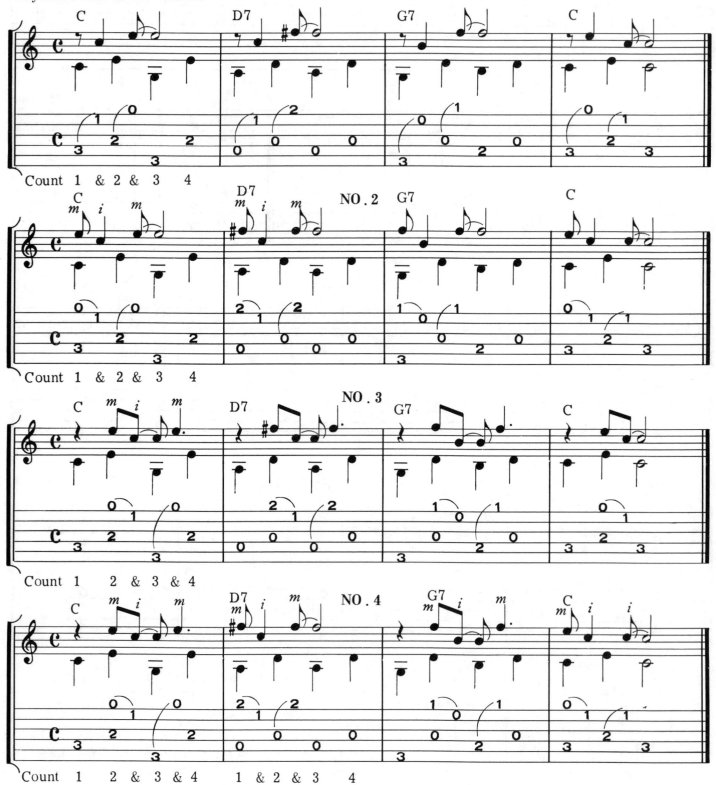

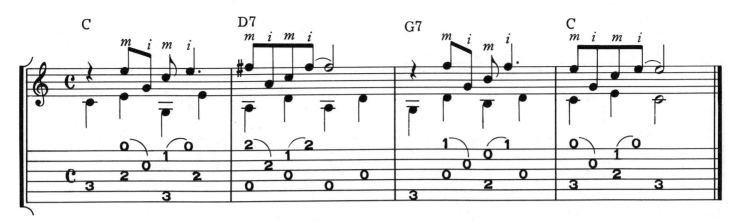

I'M ON MY WAY

Practice slowly at first to attain the feel of the syncopation. Notice the slur (hammer on) in measure number two.

In measure number eight it is not necessary to make the complete G7 chord. The first finger on "F" note on the ① string will suffice.

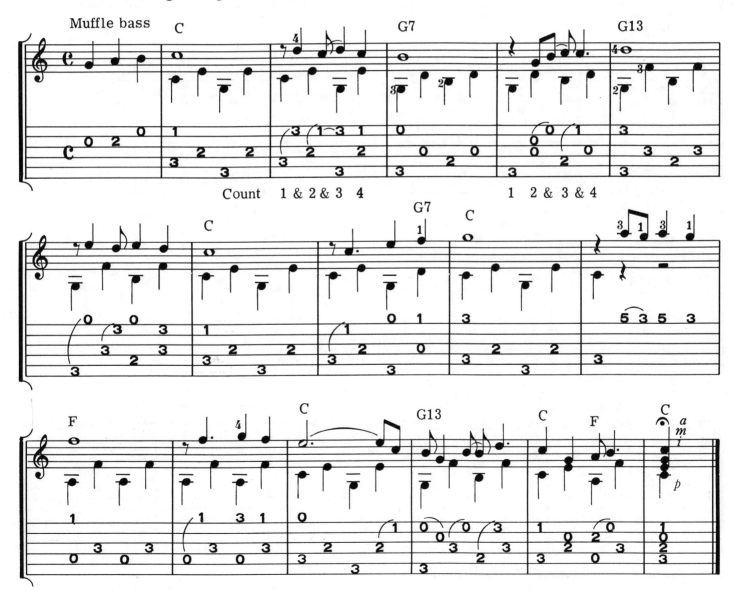

IN THE SWEET BY AND BY

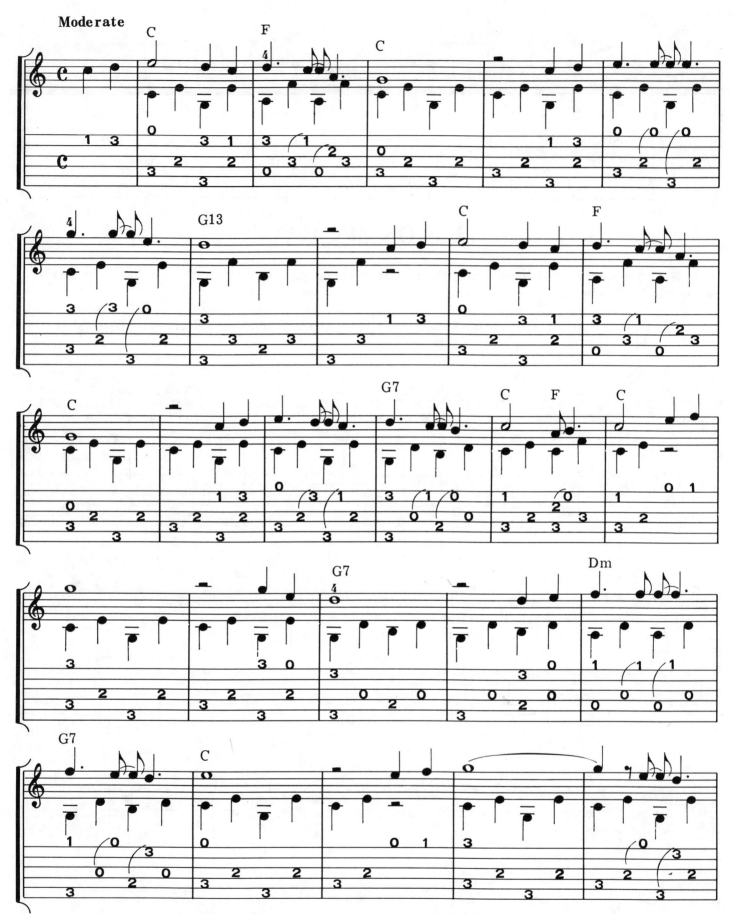

See Mel Bay's **GOSPEL GUITAR**

by Tommy Flint and Neil Griffin

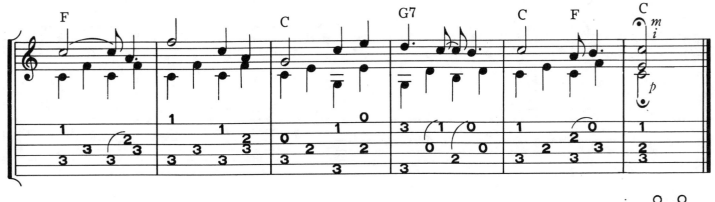

THE DRAKESBORO WAY

G13

Tommy Flint

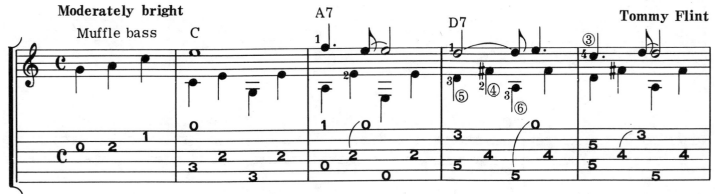

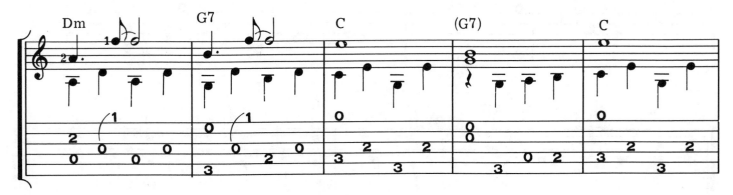

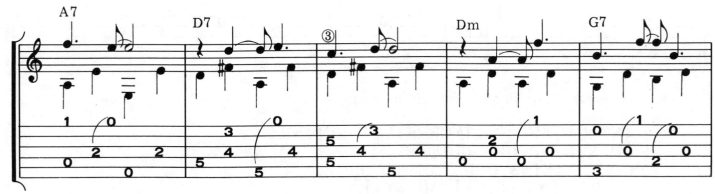

See Mel Bay's **CHET ATKINS "OFF THE RECORD"**

by Chet Atkins and Tommy Flint

Recommended material to follow this method.

ANTHOLOGY OF FINGERSTYLE GUITAR
COUNTRY BLUES GUITAR
CHET ATKINS OFF THE RECORD
MERLE TRAVIS GUITAR STYLE

from MEL BAY PUBLICATIONS